Sally-Ann Hitchcock had only just celebrated her 42nd birthday when she was diagnosed with breast cancer. Despite her diagnosis, Sally continued to be the outgoing and vivacious young woman she'd always been with an outrageous sense of humour and a captivating, infectious laugh.

A teacher, an actress, and a dear friend to so many, Sally remains an inspiration to us all.

To Sally who we miss every day.

Sally-Ann Hitchcock

THE UNINVITED GUEST

AUSTIN MACAULEY PUBLISHERS®

LONDON · CAMBRIDGE · NEW YORK · SHARJAH

A CIP catalogue record for this title is available from the British Library.

ISBN 9781035846542 (Paperback)
ISBN 9781035846559 (ePub e-book)

www.austinmacauley.com

First Published 2025
Austin Macauley Publishers Ltd®
1 Canada Square
Canary Wharf
London
E14 5AA

Thanks to Kerry Coburn for all her hard work. Without it, this book wouldn't have happened.

Table of Contents

I'm determined that I will talk about being terminally ill. I won't hide it...

Sally-Ann Hitchcock 24 September 2014

A note on the edit:

When reading Sally-Ann Hitchcock's blogs, it is impossible to miss the delight she took in spending time with friends and family. It is immediately apparent. A close second to this in the popularity stakes is a fondness for using the exclamation mark and multiple ellipses! An editor would usually rectify this enthusiasm with cuts and rewrites. But no one was going to do that to Sally's work.

It is true that there are places where tweaks have been made to correct spelling or allow necessary clarification, but these adjustments are minimal. And as painful as it is to leave in seven exclamation marks where one would do, this was done to preserve the voice and the sentiment that uttered them. Sally's voice is Sally's voice and it remains thus in the pages that follow.

Each part is different. You may notice a change in tone between them but similarly, these subtle differences reflect the person that Sally was at the time of writing. Each of you will hear and understand that.

I am afraid that there is nothing we can do to alter the ending of Sally's story. Through her telling of it, however, there is something far beyond daily events that she communicates. For one example of that, I turn to the words written by our special sunshine person, Sally-Ann Hitchcock: *31 August 2012*

I still have a way to go on my journey and will continue to keep this [blog] going, but I'm ready to now commit some of this to paper in the hope that one day it just may help someone to see the lighter side.

I hope that we all do see that lighter side; I for one am a changed person because of it.

The Guest House by Rumi

This being human is a guest house.
Every morning a new arrival.

A joy, a depression, a meanness,
Some momentary awareness comes
As an unexpected visitor.

Welcome and entertain them all!
Even if they are a crowd of sorrows,
Who violently sweep your house
Empty of its furniture,
Still, treat each guest honourably.
He may be clearing you out for
Some new delight.

The dark thought, the shame, the malice,
Meet them at the back door laughing
And invite them in.

Be grateful for whoever comes,
Because each has been sent
As a guide from beyond.

Part 1

Me…40…something! In the whole scheme of things, life has treated me pretty well. As my friend Julia used to say, "You can't empathise, you've not been through it." She was right, I hadn't. I had a great time at university, met my boyfriend straight afterwards, moved in a few years later and lived a naïve and blissful life. Don't get me wrong, I had a bit of a shopping habit which financially strained us at times, I didn't really appreciate my other half fully or what we had, but I was good company, loyal, loving and a fabulous host; even if I do say so myself! He proposed one Christmas, after 12 years of being together. I was elated, he had an affair, we got divorced and I was left heartbroken in my late 30s having to start again!

I don't want to dwell, shit happens and I'm lucky enough to have parents who have taught me to pick myself up, dust myself off and get on with it, which is exactly what I did. It wasn't easy, having just come off a big tour (I was an actress), I panicked about being financially stable and went straight back into teaching. I was lucky, I had teaching friends from before my acting days who knew I'd be committed and would do a good job and I threw myself into it wholeheartedly, gaining promotions, making fabulous friends, buying my first property and learning to manage on my own. I did it! I was successful and happy but itched for something new. At this point in my life, I felt that I'd kind of fallen into the job due to circumstances and although I wouldn't change a thing I felt I needed a new challenge and one that I had chosen. This was when a teaching job in Dubai came up. Without telling anyone, I applied, was offered an interview and got the job. Again, luck was on my side. It was perhaps the bravest thing I had ever done and for the first time in a very long time, I was excited and although I knew I would miss my friends and family incredibly I knew I could cope. You see, just as Rumi's wise words state, *everything does happen for a reason.*

What I had no idea of was what would come next. It was to be something arriving as a guest in my life, but this time, this something was really going to turn my world on its head. For the first time in my life, I would truly empathise with others. Sarah was wrong…she should have always put a 'yet' at the end of her sentence all those years ago. That's what friends do though isn't it, protect you and hope that you won't ever be able to empathise fully because you hopefully won't experience any of the rancid and horrid delights life has to offer you.

What follows is a diary of a year that took me by the horns and shook me hard. I don't profess to be a novelist, but I do hope that if you read this, it may give you some positives and some giggles if you're ever feeling low. We start the journey on Tuesday, 6 September 2011…my first day back at work after the most amazing summer celebrating a wonderful friend's wedding in Spain. The irony…

6 September 2011

"All arranged, Matt is going to let me leave early so I can come with you to the hospital. Don't worry, all will be fine xxx."

18

"Thanks, Anna, really appreciate this, meet you by the car xxx."

It was only an inset day at school, not too much to worry about. I'd told a couple of girlfriends about the niggling lump at the top of my left breast, in fact, I was supposed to have an ultrasound back in June, but the bloody insurance company had not approved it. It wasn't the first lump I'd had; one in 1996 and another in 2007, both had been nothing to worry about, 'fibro adenomas' they'd called them and they looked like black holes in the ultrasound. Textbook examples of these I was told and one hospital had actually kept the images for their own medical reference. Imagine a whole load of doctors somewhere today are probably looking right now at my tits! I thought the lump would go away in time, but it didn't. In fact, I wasn't at all worried until a very dear friend who had recently contacted me on Facebook took me for a beer in the summer holidays.

"I did some supply with a drama teacher a few years ago, she found a lump in her breast and died six months later. I've got a lump…"
"Better get it checked out then…promptly."

This friend was going to become an absolute hero to me in the up and coming months, having lost his mum to breast cancer he had a good idea of the seriousness of getting things checked out quickly, something I should have done back in June. In all fairness, I wouldn't have been quite as tanned and happy as I was on this day in September though if that had been the case. Everything happens for a reason and this was a mantra which would rule my life in the coming months.

"God, I feel a little bit nervous, Anna...this is stupid, it's just a lump, nothing to worry about."

"Yeah sure, don't worry, always best to get these things checked out though, hon."

I was called in to have my mammogram and told Anna to wait for me. The two I'd done in the past were much of a muchness, as was this one.

"Ok, Sally, I'm going to take you to have an ultrasound now. If you could lie down on the bed, take your top clothes off, cover yourself with the towel, the doctor will be with you shortly." Her English was perfect and her soft Lebanese lilt instantly put me at ease...I felt that everything was going to be fine.

"Hey, doll, let's have a look at these lumps then kid and see what we're dealing with." In contrast to the nurse, the South African doctor's accent was a little harsh, making me shuffle uncomfortably on the bed. *"Yep, looks to me like a breast cancer doll, I'm going to do a quick biopsy, but make sure you bring a friend with you when you see Dr Coach on Thursday."*

What...what...what did she just say? Did she just say she thinks I might have cancer...did she actually just say that? Without realising the tears released themselves and in big fat drops started to make my face wet.

"Don't worry doll, they'll give you chemo and radiotherapy and get rid of the cancer, you can conquer this I promise you."

What…what…what did she just say? Did she say I was going to have to have chemo? My hair…my fucking hair is going to fall out. It was at this point I started sobbing uncontrollably and they had to get Anna in from the waiting room.

It's at times like this you realise how hard it must be for your friends when you go through something like cancer. I mean, what can prepare them? There is no doubt that the look in Anna's eye said it all. She was as scared shitless at this point as I was.

The evening went by in a blur. Being an expat is a wonderful thing at a time like this and my friends rallied around making cups of tea and telling me not to worry until the biopsy results were through. We all came to the conclusion that the doctors in Dubai were different to home and that they always gave the worst-case scenario rather than looking at the positives. I hated the doctor that night…it turns out that she was an amazing woman though and her 'don't worry about it' attitude to cancer was going to be a trait I adopted and encouraged all of those around me to use. Phoning my parents was difficult.

"Well…don't worry too much darling till you have the results but you probably do have cancer! John Davenport always used to say you could tell from the ultrasound, but hey, stay positive till you know for definite."

A mother's intuition is sadly something I am unlikely to ever experience, but they know, don't ask me how but they just do!

8 September 2011

Two days back at school and all is going well. The children are settled, and everyone is happy and refreshed after their summer break…I'm talking about the staff here, not the children!

The morning goes 'tickety boo' and the school doctor (only in Dubai) very kindly agrees to come to the hospital with me for my 10.30 a.m. appointment. Today I feel calm, kind of numb to the feelings of Tuesday and more positive that perhaps things are not as bad as they appear. The hardest thing about this morning was the worried friends, in particular, three very close friends who worked alongside me in the senior school.

"Do not forget to call us…we're going to be worried about you this morning."

"Stop worrying, I told you, it's probably another of those fibroid thingy ma jigs and I'll feel like a right idiot for worrying so much."

In my head, this felt different though. Not the same as the last lumps, for a start it was bigger, harder and a longer shape. God, I wish I'd had this checked out in March when I 'think' I first felt it. It was a busy time with the school show and inspection and on top of all that I managed to get an infection in my tooth as well. I was obviously extremely run down and the lump was the last thing on my mind. In all fairness, it's one of those things that niggles you for a few hours and then your mind convinces you conveniently to forget about it and not worry. If you're sitting reading this and thinking 'I know that feeling' then for goodness sake, get yourself down the doctor and checked out…for peace of mind if nothing else. Lecture over, we all wish we'd done things we hadn't and it's time we realised life is not for regrets but for enjoying the moment and looking forward. I digress…

"Hi, take a seat…it would seem that you do indeed have breast cancer. From the biopsy, we can detect that the cancer is Grade 3 and at this point, we need to stage cancer, so I will refer you for a CT scan, blood tests and an MRI, you should have all of these in the coming days and then we will be clearer with the course of treatment you need to have. Although, at the moment, it is looking as if we might need to perform a mastectomy as we suspect the lump is quite large. My main concern at the moment is to determine whether or not the cancer has spread. You will also need a bone scan and you can have that done today, here's the form you need."

Please forgive my interpretation of this conversation…there was obviously a lot of technical vocabulary used at this time…most of which I didn't understand.

Thursday, 8 September is a bit of a blur. I remember not being incredibly upset; on reflection, I think I was probably shell-shocked more than anything. The biggest worry was telling my parents. As an only child, it's probably the worst news I have ever had to deliver to them. When I was younger, I could be a bit of a cow, but I was never in real trouble and did reasonably well making them quite proud parents. The word cancer carries so many awful connotations and telling your parents that your suspected breast cancer is indeed no longer suspected is an awful blow. I'm lucky; my parents are perhaps two of the most positive, half-full people you are ever likely to meet. Oh, they have their moans, groans and funny ways as any parent in their late sixties, or early seventies, but when things are bad, they will always see the funny side to life. Devastated as they may have felt, they never let on and told me that we'd get through the coming months, whatever that entailed.

Telling everyone else was quite a different matter. I have never in my life felt more like the Grim Reaper. While I remained upbeat (I warn you now, this wasn't always the case), everyone else took the news pretty badly. Some people had to hang up, others cried; it was, to say the least, a difficult day. I say it was hard, but I have never felt such love from people. The messages, texts, Skype calls, emails, phone calls kept coming and everyone in my life reassured me that over the coming months, they would support me. My nearest and dearest sat with me in the evening and we drank tea, watched TV and laughed about my current luck. If the previous revelations of the day had not taken place, this particular evening would have been like any other, five friends enjoying each other's company.

9 September 2011

All things considered; I slept reasonably well on Thursday night. The body is an amazing thing; if you need sleep, it will somehow help you accomplish that. Having hated biology at school, the body was now starting to fascinate me and learning more about how it was working and what it was doing was becoming my new Jane Green novel!

The girls knew me oh too well and the doorbell rang almost as instantly as I stepped out of bed. The text messages also came fast and quick with one of the funniest from my recently retired boss:

"Morning, Motherfucker…what's life thrown at you this time?"

This was a woman who knew me better than most on the humour stakes!

Fridays in Dubai are a religious day and the start of the weekend, so with a free day, the girls decided to take my mind off everything by taking me to one of our favourite haunts 'Jones the Grocers'. This was actually run by the parents of one of my most hard-working, and dare I say it, favourite pupils. It was relatively new in Dubai at this point but the food is delicious and the service absolutely amazing. If you're ever in Dubai you should definitely try it…although there is no alcohol licence in this one, for that you need to head to the Abu Dhabi branch! It was looking at the menu that caused the first of a series of 'panics' which were to haunt me over the coming days.

Having read by this point a little on the Internet about the causes of cancer and foods to eat and avoid, I stared at the menu. A hot sweat started to take over my body. What if I ate something that fuelled the cancer further? What should I avoid, what is it ok to eat? Question after question spiralled out of control in my head until Sarah, a wonderful buddy, self-taught nutrition expert and a PE teacher, took my hand and said, 'have what you want…it's all good!' Sitting there at lunch I watched my friends, was thankful for their efforts but also realised that life carries on as normal. Nothing was normal today though and the slow realisation that this horrible thing inside me was affecting everyone around me started to wash over me.

Back at the apartment, after a bit of debating we decided to watch a DVD. Something with lots of laughs, something for the life of me I can't remember. It was also a Friday night which meant people were out on the lash both in Dubai and in the UK. There were many phone calls that night and many tears. A few drinks and people became more worried about my survival from this horrible disease. As we sat watching the DVD I realised all I was doing was thinking…thinking over and over; am I going to die? When the movie finished, I turned to the girls and blurted out my thoughts:

"Do you think I'm going to die?"

"No, sweetie, no…you're going to get through this and we're going to stand by you throughout and help you get through it."

We hugged, we cried, we chatted, we drank mint tea and when I eventually told them I was tired and I was going to be ok, the girls went home.

There was one thing I knew I needed and that was as much normality in my life as possible. As wonderful as today had been, it had been an exhausting day with a lot of emotions. I am one of those annoying people that does need their own space and if I was going to get through what life was about to throw at me, there was no doubt in my mind that I simply HAD to live my life as normally as was going to be possible!

10 September 2011

I am not going to let this bloody thing get the better of me I think as I awake. I am absolutely craving my 'normal' life, life before diagnosis day, which we will now refer to as 'D Day'. I am determined to keep my life as 'normal' as possible and there is only one thing for it. I get up, put on my gym stuff and head out. *A head full of my favourite music and a good stint on the treadmill should,* I thought, *be just the tonic.* Unfortunately, though the injection from the bone scan had swollen up and my bloody arm was killing me. However hard I tried that day, normality came, but just a lot slower than I was used to.

The phone didn't stop going when I returned home, making it nearly impossible to do anything remotely quickly. The care, friendship and love shown by everyone was totally overwhelming. The nearest I can compare it to was performing the role of Mama Rose in 'Gypsy' when I was an actress. It's perhaps my favourite musical theatre role in the world and the chance to perform it was awesome. There was not a day when I came off the stage without the hugest grin on my face. The songs ran around my head like ear worms and lyrics like 'I had a dream' and 'everything's coming up roses' emulated my mood throughout the diagnosis stage.

My breast really hurt this Saturday; I can only imagine that this was totally in my head. Having found out where the cancer was, every ounce of my brain seemed to point to the lump making it impossible to forget. My dad would have been standing over me telling me not to be ridiculous if he'd been in Dubai, just as he did every time I had a bout of IBS 'it's in your head mate, stop thinking about it!'

After a hearty breakfast, I hit the shops with Anna and made some of the funniest purchases. First and foremost the 'Cancer Folder', somewhere to keep all of the information which was being thrown at me! I also purchased Lance Armstrong's autobiography; it was to be a year before I could pick this up and concentrate long enough to read it, which was a shame, as by this time, Lance was big news in the papers and media. Throughout the day, I felt relatively calm although the odd thing would agitate me; it's a weird thing isn't it, however hard you try to put something to the back of your mind, it keeps popping back like a body worm through tiredness, irritability or general grumpiness. It was a good job I had a set of friends who were incredibly patient with me and supportive during these weeks.

When I finally got home and finished doing all my chores ready for school the next day, I decided to take to my iPad and research a little bit about breast cancer. There is no doubt, this is incredibly useful and there are some amazing sites out there, but it was a lesson I was to learn that could be difficult at times. When you're given the diagnosis of cancer, it hits you like a death sentence and the more you research, the more frightened you can become. Staying strong and upbeat during moments like this is difficult and there were many times in the coming months when the iPad and I cried ourselves to sleep with the inevitable question 'what if…?'

11 September 2011

The 10-year anniversary of 9/11, as I sat in the hospital this morning watching the news (yes they have TVs and BBC

News in the hospitals in Dubai) I found myself reflecting on how different my life was ten years ago. It was my boyfriend at the time's birthday and my mum had got us tickets to see My Fair Lady with Martine McCutcheon. I remember it so well, from the news stories trickling on the TV before we left to the quietness during rush hour that welcomed us when we reached Waterloo station. I'll never forget walking across Waterloo Bridge that evening, it still remains my favourite part of London, but on that evening the traffic was minimal and nobody was talking, there was an eerie silence in the air as people contemplated their life and gave thanks that they were safe.

In the morning, I got a taxi to the hospital in order to meet the school doctor there ready for my next lot of scans and the staging of the cancer. He was the sweetest most endearing taxi driver I had come across and reminded me of Prabhakar in Gregory David Robert's brilliant novel *Shantaram*. This was a book that had been given to me by kids at school the previous July and I had very much enjoyed reading it over the summer months oblivious to the fact I had a tumour quietly growing in my breast. I was worried this morning and in usual Hitchcock style was on the toilet A LOT. Worried about school, worried about the tests, worried about the insurance cover…you name it the gremlins were hitting me hard and fast. I was right to worry about the insurance, this would be a major setback in my treatment in the future and today was the start of the problems, the MRI scan had not been approved and was therefore pushed back a day. I was not in the best frame of mind for an MRI so there was a little relief, however, I didn't realise at this time that the worry gremlins would get worse not better the following day.

The evening was great and gave me the chance I needed to catch up with myself and phone calls from home. I was feeling far more rational and could speak to people without the emotion there had been or shock when I was first diagnosed. I slept like a log that night; my body was craving sleep and gave way to a peaceful night, which was very much needed.

12 September 2011

An interesting day to say the least…I decided to go to school in the morning before the MRI. For one reason, I had my Year 11s and I was determined that this illness was not, under any circumstances going to affect their examination grades. They were perhaps one of the best classes I had ever had the privilege of teaching, they listened (any teacher reading this will understand the wow factor with this) and they wanted to succeed in a subject that quite frankly I adored. What more could you ask for? Another reason for my determination to be in school and around the kids as much as possible was because, quite frankly, it meant I was not thinking about myself!

The wait in the hospital before the MRI was not great. My stomach was flip-flopping about in its usual nervous manner meaning quick trips to the toilet were frequent. I'm one of those unfortunate people in life that suffer from IBS, or perhaps I just seem to shit a lot when I'm nervous…whichever, it's a pain in the backside (excuse the pun) and this morning was no different.

"Come through, Miss Sally." It was the norm in Dubai to be called your first name rather than your surname, something quite sweet and I definitely miss it now I'm back in Blighty.

"If you'd like to put the gown on, buttons at the front and sit on the bed, until we're ready for you." I did as the nurse said and plonked myself on the edge of the bed. Swinging my legs I could feel the nerves building again and for fear of needing another trip to the loo, I decided to push the curtain aside slowly so I could see what was going on outside the cubicle, and in order to take my mind of the impending MRI machine. This was probably the worst mistake I was going to make today. I had a clear view of the MRI room from the gap in the curtain and to my absolute horror watched the doctor telling two of the radiographers off. The Arabic nature can be quite harsh at times and this doctor was not holding back. From three different nationalities, they all spoke in pigeon English. The crux of the telling-off was that the guy in front of me had had a cardiac arrest in the MRI machine. No wonder I had waited nearly an hour for my turn.

"Fuck…oh fuckedy, fuckedy, fuck!"

My legs had started to swing at a ridiculously fast pace over the side of the bed and in true Hitchcock style, I had started humming. Something I always did when scared. It got me down a rather large slope in Chatel years previously, it was either singing or crapping myself and the same feelings were building up inside me again.

With that, the curtain whipped back and the radiographer called me into the MRI room. Not only was I faced with the machine of doom but I also had to have a line put into me so that they could feed some contrast dye into my bloodstream half way through the scan. On top of that, I was asked to lie face down and stick my boobs into what I can only describe as a couple of plastic buckets, resting my head on a pillow. The whole process was less than glamorous and in a Muslim country trying to manoeuvre yourself in this fashion with the door open, was anything but appropriate. I was then asked if I'd like to listen to music. I had had an MRI scan once before in my life to look at an odd swelling behind one of my eyes. It turned out that there was nothing wrong with me, but I remember clearly the soothing tones of Capital Radio, helped see me through the experience. When given the choice of music, I chose Snow Patrol. It was a band I liked immensely although interestingly, at the time, I didn't know I would be watching them, bald, later on in the year!

Snow Patrol was perhaps not the best choice of music. As I entered the MRI machine, with my face planted down on a pillow and my breasts firmly in place in the 'buckets', a wave of fear and panic took over me. I think this was probably the first time that I had properly realised what was happening to me. I had cancer! There was no denying it and this god-awful machine was about to detect whether I was going to live or die, it was that simple. God, I so didn't want to die. I was 41 for god's sake, I liked life, I liked my job, and I loved my family and friends…what the hell was going to happen to me? After the first 10-minute scan I could stay in the machine no longer and pressed the panic button! The radiographers slid the bed out from its space-age tube and came in to check I was ok. I told them I was feeling claustrophobic, so they readjusted my head on the pillow and for a few seconds I felt ok and they slid me back in for scan number two. For some reason, I think they felt that playing the music in my ears louder might help me, but being the drama queen I am I was suddenly imagining myself on a movie set, dying and living the last hours of my life…dramatic I know, but the truth is all the same. Again, I pressed the panic button.

Miss Sally, we really have to do the scan and you need to stay in the machine, we can't keep pulling you out every time you press the panic button. "Erm, excuse me, you told me to press the bloody button if I needed to!" It was at this point that I started crying…I mean really crying. The radiographers were quite sweet I suppose, but they had a time scale and I on top of the bloke who had had the cardiac arrest was now causing mayhem to their daily schedule.

"Ok, ok, I'll try again…"

Back in I went.

"Oh fuck, I'm going to die…I'm not even in England, oh shit…I'm really going to die." I pressed the panic button, but this time, over the speaker into the room came a voice saying, "It's ok, Miss Sally, not long now!"

"OK, is it fuck ok! I am not staying in this machine a moment longer!"

It was at this point I was not to behave in my finest manner and decided there was only one thing for it; I crawled out of the MRI machine. Needless to say, the buckets got stuck around my breasts, the stand holding the drip fell over and as I climbed out I fell straight onto my arse on the floor, legs a kimbo and breasts in full view of anyone who fancied a butcher's!

The nurses called my friend who was in the waiting room (Farina, the school doctor) and I was to find out later that I had, had my first panic attack! It was a ridiculous feeling; I was crying uncontrollably and felt hot and breathless. If it wasn't the cancer that was going to kill me, this might! Luckily, Farina managed to calm me down enough to explain to me how important this scan was in my life. After chatting with the nurses, it was decided that Farina would come in with

33

me and hold my hand (this was possible if I entered in a superman-style position with my hands above me out of the machine). The simple motion of someone holding your hand and telling you that you were doing really well and there wasn't long left made the process bearable. To this day, I will never be able to thank my friend enough…if I had been on my own in the hospital; it is quite probable that the MRI would never have taken place. It was the nightmare of this day that made me realise something very important in my treatment. I needed my mum and dad! As old and brave as I thought I was, I needed to be home right now and needed a little bit of good old British reassurance that everything would be fine. The decisions I was making in my head while all of this was going on were going to be some of the biggest and best choices I could have possibly made and in effect were about to save my life! Everything happens for a reason!

Farina (not just the school doctor but a very good friend) continued to be amazing, she answered all those tricky medical questions that no one else could and constantly translated the technical spiel after every appointment. The MRI and further blood tests went well and were relatively quick, allowing me to get back to school and dare I say it back to normality. Kids are amazing, they are needy and quite rightly concerned about themselves and they will never know how much they were the saving grace in my treatment.

Tuesday 13 September

This was perhaps one of the most normal days I'd had in what felt like a long time. A full day of teaching and sorting children and their problems out. Just what the doctor ordered so to speak. It's funny, when I split with my husband five years previously I went straight from the stage back to teaching. It is a job I love and one in which you have literally no time to think about or feel sorry for yourself. If you've ever found yourself dwelling on your own problems a little too much, it is a career I would thoroughly recommend. Don't get me wrong, it is by no means an easy job, but seeing children succeed and helping them realise their ambitions and dreams is an amazing feeling. These children and their parents played a huge, huge part in the year to come and when I eventually left Dubai in 2012, there were a lot of tears shed from all parties.

There were a few unusual and important occurrences that happened on this day though. Even though I was particularly busy at work, there was an underlying feeling of fear and dread for the results tomorrow. The most important thing I still didn't know was whether the cancer had actually spread at all. Not knowing whether you have the chance of life or death is a strange feeling…I hate to say it, but it makes you appreciate life and all that you have taken for granted for so long.

Wednesday 14 September

In my typical style and the only way I was starting to feel I could get through each day, I went to school and taught my IGCSE kids. It gave me a purpose each morning, a reason to get out of bed…a reason, if you like, to live.

Farina came with me to another appointment. There were two reasons for this. One, she was an amazing lady, had become a good friend and cared for me at this difficult time. The other was quite simple, she was a doctor and what I couldn't understand, she could. I also felt that, with her in the room, my breast consultant would be truthful with me.

The fact I had breast cancer was no shock, this had been clearly told to me last week. The grade of the cancer being Grade 3 meant it was aggressive and, more worryingly, fast-growing. The cancer had not spread further from what they could see (thank god) and my options were clearly laid out in front of me:

1. I would need a double (bilateral) mastectomy.
2. I could have reconstructive surgery at the same time, although this was something they would not be able to do in Dubai (at this point I wanted to have everything done in Dubai to save the time off work).
3. If I didn't have reconstructive surgery, I could have implants put in after all my treatment.
4. I would definitely have chemo.

"I won't lose my hair…I'll wear one of those cold cap things."

"Sally, you must realise that cancer is a very individual disease, just because one of your friends didn't lose their hair, doesn't mean you won't. You have to realise that your body will react differently to others."

The consultant's words hit me like a barge pole. The hair thing was becoming a huge issue for me and something I was starting to obsess about on a daily basis.

1. I would have to have radiotherapy after the chemotherapy.
2. I would be in treatment for the next 9 months.

Nine months…September, October, November, December, January, February, March, April, May! May! Are you having a bloody laugh!!!!!? That's nearly a whole school year. As a teacher, you stop measuring your year from January to December but rather from September to August.

After the last consultation, I was very sure of one thing. I wanted reconstruction straight away. I had been warned of the risk of this, but the thought of feeling not like a woman and having to cope with that as well as the cancer was too much for me. If it killed me, then so be it. I still had choices to make and I was not going to let the cancer take those away from me. In actual fact, the decision to have the reconstruction meant I had no choice but to go home and this was a huge relief. I definitely needed my parents at this point, a little bit of home and to have a big hug. This really was one of my better decisions.

Interval

The following days went by in a blur. I carried on working, I went to the gym, and I went out with friends and generally behaved as though nothing were wrong. In the background, I was arranging appointments, hospital visits, breast consultants and reconstructive surgeons in the UK. I had been asked at one point to take a picture of my breasts and my body for the reconstructive surgeon. It was these funny moments that kept me going…asking my friend Anna to take the photos as I stood in the living room in nothing but my knickers. The whole thing was providing plenty of giggles, that's for sure.

This 'in-between' time also gave me a lot of opportunity to reflect. I had spent so many years now moaning about the fact my marriage had broken down and how unlucky I was on this front; I had forgotten to live for the day. I started to appreciate every sight around me, the sunrise, the sunset, the beach, the birds…you name it, and I couldn't get enough of it. My camera started to come everywhere with me, I would wake up, see the sunrise from my balcony and take a picture of it. I wanted to appreciate every day, but most importantly, I wanted to live.

22 September 2011

Being in Dubai meant things were a little trickier than usual. I didn't want to come home until just before the operation; I wanted this normality I was craving to last for as long as possible. I'm sure a lot of people felt I was in denial. This wasn't the case though; I was talking things through with some really dear friends on a daily basis. Thank god they never grew tired of listening to me going on!

My first consultation with my reconstructive surgeon took place on Skype. This wonderful man who I will refer to as JC never ceased to amaze me! Anyhow, in true JC style, there was me on Skype chatting away about the reconstructive surgery I would be having.

"Can you show me your stomach, Sally-Ann?"

I did this, and he said he felt there was not enough fat on my stomach to make a double reconstruction. Now, I wish this were the case, but at the time I had enough fat on my stomach to feed a large family. I wobbled it a bit to show him but he still shook his head and said he may need to take some from my bottom. This in itself was hilarious, and once I showed JC my flat arse, he agreed that that might be a problem. My flat arse had been the butt (excuse the pun) of many a joke. When my god daughter was little she asked me why my bottom was on my stomach…got to love children for their honesty sometimes. The Skype conversation ended with JC saying he would wait to make a decision when we met in a couple of weeks' time.

Retelling my friend Jo the story of the Skype conversation later in the evening, I found myself rolling on the floor laughing. She couldn't believe I had actually wobbled my stomach on camera in order to prove its flabbiness and quite frankly, neither could I. What on earth must JC have thought of me…perhaps I was a mad, mad woman after all!

Part 2

13 October 2011

This is where I am, McIndoe Surgical at the Queen Victoria Hospital. Go to the Contact page for the address if you are coming to visit. It's about 20 minutes from Junction 10 on the M23.

13 October 2011

Hey, everyone…thought this might be a good way to keep you up to date. Rough as a dog today, got up twice, but passed out…whoops…thought I'd be alright. Apparently, tomorrow I'll feel a bit better and so on. Eight-hour op, so pretty big, but all for the right reasons.

Thank you for all your cards, texts, flowers and balloons. I am feeling the love and already have a reputation for being a chatterbox. Oh! And btw, Kylie's nurse was my nurse last night…loving that! Xxx

14 October 2011

Hey, Everyone. This is a little page/blog so we can keep in touch and I can tell you how I'm doing. It's a private group so it's just for us.

15 October 2011

Day 3…On sleeping tablets at the moment which is much needed and means I'm getting a good six to seven hours sleep. Feel rough, but can't help thinking I'm just a little bit scared, having never been immobilised before it's just a bit frightening. Catheter and hopefully two more drains out today which will make sitting up a bit easier :-). Fingers crossed today starts to see improvements. Thank you sooo much for all your kind messages, cards, visits, flowers and pressies! I could not get through this without all of your love and support xxx. Oh…And my arse is bloody killing me!!

P.s copped a look yesterday and not bad people…not bad! Alastair…you'll have to join the queue;-)

16 October 2011

Day Four in the hospital!!! Had to get up for a pee this morning hence it's a bit early. After a crap morning with lots of tears and generally feeling very sorry for myself, I had a good day yesterday! I am now walking (assisted) and can stand up (on my own). This is a huge accomplishment and is going some way to relieving that arse ache :-). Had lots of lovely visitors yesterday and my room is now known as the party room. Miss you guys in Dubai masses but so many of you called yesterday which made my day (Anna and Rhian I will get you back for calling poolside!). Had a shower yesterday, the naturally drying hair is not a good look; quite frankly I look bloody awful! I am doing my entire physio and really trying hard to make a speedy recovery. I only have two drains left which is fab, they are horrible to look at and quite frankly make me want to vomit so goodness knows how they make my visitors feel. It really is times like this that you realise how lucky you are, and I know I am blessed with the bestest friends worldwide! I have had lots of laughing and in true Hitchcock style have a funny story to tell you about my mum, not appropriate for here but needless to say I nearly wet my pants (nice netted ones too) and nearly burst some stitches…V funny. Loads of love to you all.

17 October 2011

Day Five in the Hitchcock Hospital Bed (said with a big Welsh BB accent!)

Another early start…can't seem to sleep past 4.30, despite the very good sleeping tablets. I think I'm a nurse and dropped from two to one last night and slept for the same amount of time. It takes a little while to coordinate drains and move myself to go for a pee so by the time I actually get there I'm wide awake!

Had a great day yesterday, showered, and dressed in my own clothes then walked up and down the corridor carrying my drains in a pillowcase holding onto the lovely Alan. My cackle has disappeared and unfortunately, I have developed a rather disturbing laugh while holding on to my tummy so as not to burst the stitches! I am without doubt recovering though and I couldn't have imagined a few days ago feeling more human. Amanda even came and straightened my hair in the afternoon (after her half marathon) so I even looked a bit more normal!

So, things are definitely on the up. One more drain came out yesterday so more gas and air. After initially not liking this, I'm now thinking I'm some kind of stand-up on it! Saturday night was a revelation as Johnny from The X Factor was singing as I was having a drain out while on gas and air…I was literally shouting at the TV 'will you shut up sounding like a bloody woman!' There were a few expletives I've kept out.

So, 5.25 a.m. and I'm ready for a new day and hopefully even more improvements! Despite the fact, I feel brill and I'm doing brilliantly, due to the last drain and the fact I have to go back to the theatre on Wednesday (not the showbiz kind), it is looking like I'll be here till Friday…boo! You'll be pleased to hear the arse is making a good recovery from getting up and moving. Much love and big hugs to you all. In the words of Karen and Paul last night…it is you guys and your encouragement that is getting me through this…and of course the opportunity to write all about me every day, wish I'd taken this hobby up years ago.

17 October 2011

I've just written a message and it's disappeared…It was for the Dubai people who have left me speechless. It goes without saying how much I love you all from the bottom of my heart, but I am totally overwhelmed. Sitting here with my parents absolutely dumbstruck! I just don't know what to say.

18 October 2011

P.s if I've missed someone off the blog that you think might want to read my whinging please feel free to add, a lovely person set this up for me when I was a bit out of it Thursday so I'm bound to have made some mistakes. Much love, you fabulous people!

18 October 2011

Day Six in the Hitchcock House said with a Geordie accent…Went downhill a bit last night, weepy, high temp and bloody drain in the reconstructed breast is killing me! Back on morphine this morning! It just makes you feel miserable! Plus points are I went back to two sleeping pills and slept much better! My right arm is like a dead weight, I'm doing my entire physio etc., but apparently, this is to be expected so I've just got to suck it up and see. Had a lovely time with the lovely Katie and Helen during the day, poor folks though they get the crap of me. After they left last night, I was very teary…just want to feel normal again. The look is fine, that is not upsetting me at all but the pain and carrying this frigging drain around with me is giving me the right ache! Today is a new day…the nurses have told me I'll be up and down, you've all told me that too…do I listen…do I f**k.

Sending big hugs to you all and I will get through this!

19 October 2011

Morning! Thinking of you. Bye, bloody drain! Xxx

Just found out I'm not going in until early afternoon because I'm a 'dirty' patient…Can you believe it! Apparently, a clean patient is a first op and a dirty patient is one who is going back into theatre where there is more risk of infection! My rather gorgeous surgeon also popped in this morning to have a peek and explain what he's going to do this afternoon. He also told me, 'They look better, much better than those big old knockers you had!' ha! The reconstructed one is a little bit bigger so a bit of fat will come out of that today. Feeling so much chirpier today but the thought of another op is not appealing in the slightest! My poor, poor body! Well, roll on the face lift and the boob augmentation in front of me (I kid you not...) and let's get on with it. Much love and I can't even begin to tell you how much your messages brighten up my day!

19 October 2011

Later—still waiting to go down for the op, feeling rubbish and then I get this beautiful picture. I feel all American but seriously you guys get me through every day right now.

Day Seven in the MacIndoe Surgical Centre! Day Seven! (said by the very good-looking BB man—obv going to be gay then). Get Me out of here (said by Ant and Dec)!

Ok, third op in two weeks today...not bad going for someone who's never been in the hospital before. They are going to tidy up the reconstruction today and take the extra flap out (terminology just sounds great, hey) as well as remove the final drain which is quite frankly making me miserable!

Managed to cheer up yesterday you'll be pleased to hear but am seriously exhausted! The doctor said that my body is working so hard to recover it is doing the equivalent of a half marathon every day...don't be jealous Anna;-). Well hopefully, they will let me out tomorrow or at the absolute latest Friday, I can't wait!

Big hugs and lots of love to you all...looking forward to the scars healing and getting my bikini back on...then I remember I might have the baldness to contend with...bloody, bloody cancer, will be on the lookout for a fetching swim cap;)

20 October 2011

Just saw my dishy surgeon :-) I'm going home to mum and dad's today :-) Happy.com!

20 October 2011

Day Eight in the Hitchcock Hospital! I slept without a sleeping tablet for six and half hours only being woken once by the facelift vomming in the room across the hall...Go me! Op yesterday went well although I ended up not going in until 5 pm and drove my poor folks crazy with my huffing and puffing and need to go to the toilet 100 times. The drain is now gone, but there is still a lot of swelling on the reconstruction arm pit...looks like I've got a rugby ball stuffed there but things on the whole are good.

I will miss all the wonderful care I've had here. My last night and I was looked after by Kylie's nurse again so a good end to the stay.

My only downside of yesterday was receiving a call from Maidstone Hospital telling me I had a bone scan! This has properly stressed me out because I had one in Dubai and of course am questioning why I have to go back! I will try and speak to the breast surgeon to find out! I've decided that this is the bloody problem with cancer, you get over one hurdle, start to feel happy and then get knocked again with something else! The months ahead are going to be an experience, I know that...god I feel for everyone who has or has to go through this in their life. I've also been given the chat about not being fixated on losing my hair! I need Michael Cooper to explain to them that the scarf look will just not work with a moon face! Anyway, moan over. On the whole, yesterday was positive and if I'm back at my folks nine days after coming here instead of ten, I'm pleased…You know me…Like to get the competitive streak going :-)

Miss you all oodles.

21 October 2011

So, yesterday was 'discharge' day…so beautifully named by my friend Karen! Being home is lovely but terribly frightening at the same time. Not being particularly good with blood and gore when going to bed last night instead of ringing a bell all I could do was sort of gag and try my hardest to do a bodge job to see me through the night…Nice! The scars seem to have blistered which is very normal but of course, they ooze a little eeeerrrrggghhh!

Mum and Dad love having me home and really can't do enough for me, I'm frustrated as hell as everything is taking about 10 times longer and you all know me well enough to know that patience is not my strongest virtue.

Had the most bizarre dream about teaching in my hospital gown! Not quite sure what that says! It's looking like I've got to go through the whole scanning/testing thing again; i.e., the second time of the 'has it spread'. So, not looking forward to this again, especially as now have time to dwell and no teaching to take my mind off everything. Ho hum… I have my box of good luck with me and, really, can things have changed in five weeks?

Well for today I will mostly be catching up on all the TV I Skyped at my parent's while in Dubai.

Still missing you masses and loved my little pics of Sarah, Iwiyisi and Ernie out last night…I hope there was a dolly roll in there somewhere.

22 October 2011

Things I thought I'd never be doing at 41: waking up my parents because I have blood coming from my drain hole...I kid you not! I'm passing out, my lovely ma aged 68 is cool as a cucumber and sorting it—dad stays where he is and shouts instructions from the bedroom! Only in Hitchcock's world! Looks like it's back to the hospital tomorrow!

23 October 2011

So, back to the hospital yesterday to sort out the drain holes! I now have a little bag attached to my right boob to collect gross-looking gunk which I have named JC after my rather dishy surgeon...JC and I had our first outing yesterday to M & S on the way home from the hospital. Just a quick coffee and the purchase of some control pants to keep my back in kilter and stop me hunching! I was considerably slower than anyone else in the shop but hey, I managed an hour out being very closely monitored by the folks.

The hospital has told me to remember I've had major surgery and JC (surgeon not bag) has given my mum strict instructions to bully me to rest!

Have managed to finish the first series of 'Luther!' Will bring it back to Dubai, people...it is fabulous!

It's all about the roast dinner today :-)

Big hugs from me and JC (the bag this time not the surgeon).

25 October 2011

Bit late on the update today. Been to see the breast surgeon and get the results from the tumour! Well...it was very large, we knew that. It was Grade 3, very aggressive, not so good! It hasn't spread to the lymph nodes only a microscopic amount in the sentinel node…bloody miracle and makes me one hell of a lucky girl. Because they had already staged it in Dubai we know it hasn't spread which again is a miracle. The cancer has no relation to my hormones or something else which I can't remember (info overload) and it hasn't run in my family so they are a little perplexed as to why I have it. There is the possibility that I could be the first gene carrier and they will test for this. I've now been referred to an oncologist closer to home and will probably speak to him in the next week, they are keen that I start my chemo ASAP!

I've decided that I will do everything in my power not to lose my hair but if I do I will buy myself a pair of Manolo Blahniks and wear them with style…this will not bring me down! Anyhow, the further down the line the treatment, the closer I am to getting back to Dubai and full health. Everything happens for a reason; I have no idea why at the mo, but I'll find out eventually. I am still springing leaks so on antibiotics now as well…still smiling and laughing though. Was told off today for over doing it by the doc… Not quite sure what part of sitting on my fat arse and watching box sets is overdoing it but I will try harder! Lots of love everyone.

25 October 2011

Only gone and sprung another leak! Bit of a crisis in the Hitchcock House tonight but patched up and ready for another trip to the hospital tomorrow! Would be ok if the hospital wasn't an hour's drive away! Oh well…another morning with my dishy surgeon, got to look at the positives :-). Have had a fab day with the lovely Amanda and have been well looked after…and still being told to rest. I am doing nothing people I tell you—what is rest? Taking JC and m' leaks to bed early tonight, oh how glamorous my life has become…xxx

26 October 2011

Definition of a bodge job…Waking up in the middle of the night with the leaks and thinking shit, how am I going to sort this out? I know, put sanitary towels across my tummy. Genius! I kid you not! My life is so far removed from four weeks ago it is unbelievable! Back to the hospital, we go…again! Oh! The cat's puked too: super morning and it's only 5.52 a.m.!

27 October 2011

Ok new bag to add to the collection on the tummy, to be known as SB friends with JC! This bag is particularly nice as you can see it through my trousers adding to my attractiveness levels, not embarrassed at all…much! The nurse was most impressed with my quick thinking on the dressing front and then was a little shocked when my ooze made a run for it and exploded over the floor, absolute truth I promise you!

27 October 2011

No leaks! Hoorah! Two great big frigging bags hanging off me, but last night ladies and gentlemen, I remained leak free :-). My next task is to get my skinny jeans back on, this means SB the tummy bag has got to go. I am starting to get a little fed up with the joggers look and rocking that with a great big bag showing through is really not working!! Other good news is my oldest girlfriend Wendy came round last night and helped me de-fuzz my armpits…Dubai peeps you have all these luxuries to come I'm telling you;-).

Oh and one more thing, my ma has developed a crush on the surgeon! She and my aunty were ogling him in the hospital yesterday…He left my hospital room via the secret door—no idea what he was scared of! Hahahaha hilarious!

28 October 2011

Today I am feeling totally overwhelmed. Thank you to all the amazing people in Dubai who did the breast cancer walks this morning! You guys are totally amazing and when I kick this thing, I will be spending serious amounts of my energy fundraising! I found out this week I have triple-negative breast cancer which is one of the rarer forms and tends to be more aggressive. It's most common in Hispanic and African American women or women who have a history of breast cancer in the family. Goodness knows how I've got it, always got to be different hey! I did a bit of Internet research on it last night and then wished I hadn't! Anyhow, what I'm trying to say is because it's a relatively new find it's where lots of the cancer research money is going, so every day my chances are increasing! Well, if the critters think they can mess with the Hitch, they have another thing coming!

Back to the hospital again today for some more leakage patching. Have a great brunch, Dubai people, man I wish I was having a few drinks with you all today. Big hugs from an overwhelmed and totally grateful buddy whose hair looks like a monkey's been at it and who can't get her skinny jeans on yet!

29 October 2011

Today marks my first proper outing…I'm off to Helen and Richard's for some X Factor and am very excited! Got to disguise the bag collecting crap from my tummy and all will be well! Being picked up and taken home, I'm like a little old lady. Am defo quicker on my feet and the right side of my body is healing quicker than the left—awkward my dad calls me; he could well be right!

31 October 2011

First outing out = bloody lovely! Thank you, guys for looking after me! Oh, how lovely to feel a little bit human for the evening! I love Little Mix, Misha B and dare I say, Kitty! The girls are ruling X Factor this year!

31 October 2011

Only Lizzie Petrie aka my little sister can get away with sending me a swimming hat and an eyebrow pencil in the post…as well as lots of other gorgeous goodies pmsl! Back to see dishy consultant JC today so he can tell me how gorgeous I am…Swelling is not looking great on the reconstructed side…Looks like my boob goes under my armpit-truth! JC assures me that the radiotherapy will shrink it a bit and a bit of Lypo after my treatment will sort out any problems! My god! I'm sounding more like Jordan by the day! The leaking is getting better on a daily basis and I'm hoping that SB the tummy bag will come off this week, if not today. This could mean the appearance of skinny jeans, fingers crossed! Feeling more and more human on a daily basis, mostly thanks to all of you wonderful people, who keep my spirits up. Just waiting for the oncologist to get in touch and then the start of the dreaded chemo—don't mind admitting I'm absolutely shitting myself about this part on so many levels. It was the same with the anaesthetic but I got through that. Somehow will get through the next step! Sending lots of Monday love to you all.

1 November 2011

SB has been removed! I am bag-free :-). Fingers crossed for no leakage and I can go for small walks! JC (dishy surgeon) is very happy with me, although thought I was slightly odd when I told him I'd been scaring people with my swollen bits at the weekend—can't think why? I am a very happy bunny, still look like a patchwork quilt with dressings everywhere but to say goodbye to the juice bags is definitely a good thing. Happy Halloween, any kid who knocks on this door could get more than they bargained for;-). Xxxx

2 November 2011

Last night I managed seven hours of sleep-miracle! The longest sleep I've had since the 10 October unless you include the nine-hour operation sleep that is! Today I showered without anyone in the house! I also changed all my dressings without gagging! Now this may all seem very trivial but one small step for mankind is one huge step for Sally-Ann! A few weeks ago, I couldn't even look at my scars without gagging and making stupid faces…see everything happens for a reason—welcome nurse Sally!

4 November 2011

Lovely morning…Cat comes and sits on my bed purring away…Gets up leaving a turd! Cheers Chelsea (I didn't name her). How's your luck?! I thought I was the patient!

5 November 2011

So today is my first trip away, two nights in Chichester with the lovely Hammonds! Yippee, am hoping for no leaks—to quote Bella...*You don't have bags, excellent; you won't leak on my bed.*

Bella is impressed with the way I'm looking, she thinks I look much better with my smaller boobs and flat stomach, I quote, *you look much better, like you've been rolled over by a roller.*

Only the Hammond family! Ben is finding the concept of me telling him my stomach is now my boob a little difficult to grasp, I am realising there are some things you just don't tell children. I warned you all...that this is a learning curve.

Have a lovely weekend everyone.

7 November 2011

A lovely weekend with lovely friends! Totally ruined by the NHS refusing to treat me with chemo...can you effing believe it! So glad I've been a law-abiding citizen all these years! Stressed-out parents, stressed-out Sally...Great way to clear constipation though!

8 November 2011

Ok...stinking letter written to NHS looks like I should be entitled to treatment according to the Department of Health. However, it is the discretion of the hospital so have tried to word my email in a charming manner! We shall see. New news today. I've discovered nursing pads...just as good as a sanitary towel for the booby leakage, but better shaped and with the added bonus of a nipple, and very handy when you're missing one. Can't wait to show the nurse my new invention on Wednesday…dishy surgeon will probably think I've lost the plot completely :-). I have spent most of today on the email and phone, stressing about the chemo and as a result have sprung two leaks and am bloody knackered. Sitting with my dad watching 'Wheeler Dealers' and finding I've got a bit of a crush on the mechanic, good way to end the day.

Big thanks to all the people I have ranted at over the last 24 hours and thank you for putting up with me, I am dragging that positivity up from somewhere still I tell you!

Wig shopping tomorrow with the lovely Emma and Hels…feeling strangely excited at the prospect of having lovely hair…we are all aware that the scarf look does not suit the moon face. Fingers crossed I find one or two, just in case. Hopefully, I'll find out in the next couple of days if the NHS will treat me and if not I have some big decisions to make about what to do…I feel like my brain is about to explode, anything for a quiet life. Love you all lots!

9 November 2011

Today is a good day! Two wigs purchased, one blonde, one red and with the necessary help of two amazing friends! I don't mind admitting that I very nearly cried when I realised a wig looks quite a lot like a wig, whatever the style! I am well chuffed with them and even more so because they were cheaper because of the cancer and on top of that I can now have a whole load of free treatments at Harrods! Vicki Ullah could not have been lovelier and Em and Hels could not have been more patient! On top of that, Frank Lampard was sat just by us while we were in the wig department and Colin Jackson (he's gorgeous) was at the tube! Michael, I've bought a scarf too, the same as Kylie's; you have permission to piss yourselves, I still look like a moon face!

I have also heard from the NHS and it looks like they are going to treat me! One more document to be supplied and an apology for the distress! Hooray, it seems there is justice! The woman in Harrods had recommended I go to a magazine! I am considering, however, offering my blog to one, what do you reckon, totally selfish or perhaps comforting for someone who may well be going through the same thing as me? Thoughts on a postcard! Back to the hospital tomorrow to see the dishy JC with my nursing pads! Considering the circumstances life is not bad, I am blessed with the most amazing friends and family…and I will never take another day for granted! Everything happens for a reason.

9 November 2011

A sneak peek and a huge thank you to the cancer fairies. You know who you are.

The NHS…they say yes! Appointment with the oncologist on the 15 November! Now to really shit my pants for the next scary part of the journey! Please let my first chemo be before the 25 November so I can go to the seaside to recuperate on the 28th!

11 November 2011

This evening I am going back to my previous school to watch the Drama Festival that I started up in 2007…Really excited to see this still running and develop further within the school. This will be my first proper evening trip out so I'm hoping Amanda saves us a chair at the end of the row near a door just in case;-). Fingers crossed all will be fine.

I've been called many things in the past, idiot, loser, dumb ass, shitcock, and pitchfork and more recently 'dim-witted' (this one was even published! Charming). Last night I proved all of these correct by announcing the wrong fricking result at a Drama Festival...what an arse and how embarrassing! Luckily, it was for the 'best choice of play' so not the overall winner! Still felt like an absolute div!

The Drama Festival was brill, a lovely evening with some great mates and lots of giggles. I feel so proud of myself to have started this at Rosebery School in 2007 and that it is still growing and developing as a worthwhile event in the school calendar, I keep saying it...but there is a reason for everything and had I been well I would not have been able to share in last night's occasion!

My friends last night couldn't believe how well I looked...It is bizarre of course as I do just look like me! I did remind them that my stomach is now my boob and should they have the pleasure of seeing me naked they prob wouldn't be quite so impressed. Recorded 'Life's Too Short' the new Ricky Gervais series with the lovely Warwick Davies (did I tell you I did Snow White with him when I was in the business...?). So, going to enjoy that with my cuppa and toast now! Have a lovely day everyone.

12 November 2011

Bit sore this morning...on the reconstructed side. Now here's the problem; I shouldn't have any feeling there so I'm either imagining it, or another little miracle is occurring in my body and it's sore = healing right! JC was his usual charming self yesterday, very impressed with my nursing pad idea but he is totally Movembering right now. I am seeing him again in ten days and I'm telling you now he is going to be one hairy man by that stage! Makes me feel slightly better as not been able to keep myself as groomed as usual of late (prob more info than you needed—sorry!).

Oooh meant to say that, got told yesterday by JC I was an absolutely model patient who recovers well and has a high pain threshold...get me! He then told Sandy the lovely nurse to pick my scabs off! Pick my scabs! Are you having a laugh? I have not touched one scab! And there she was picking the loose ones. No wonder I'm bloody sore!

I have a little message for Alastair this morning...drains = bottles hanging from tubes connected to my inners which fill with...erm how can I put this...inner juice! Can't wait to explain this in graphic detail to you Ernie;-).

Hope I haven't put you all off your breakfasts/lunch but thought today's post should be written in true Hitchcock style with all the gory bits. Lots of love everyone and Dubai peeps I miss you, Anna please run round my flat and tell my stuff I miss it...do not borrow my clothes.

;-). Love ya!

12 November 2011

A little bit of Dubai in London...lunch with the lovely Niamh, if we were in flip flops rather than boots and coats, we could have been back at home! And lunch in a Moroccan organic cafe-perfect!

First day without painkillers...thought it was time to give it a go; so far, so good! Apart from the fact I can't fly, take about two hours to get ready (am a dab hand at the dressing malarky now though), and can't last too long without getting knackered...I'm feeling pretty much back to my old self :-).

12 November 2011

Cup of tea, strictly[1] then X Factor and a gingerbread man thanks to Dawn and Sam…Pig in shit springs to mind :-).

14 November 2011

Thought for the day…had to succumb to the pain killers at the end of the day but more so for period pains (sorry boys) rather than pain from the op. Now here's the question…I have been having an aching pain on my reconstructed side over the last few days, my stomach is now my boob so does that mean I now get period pains in my boob? Makes you wonder, doesn't it? Have a lovely day…

16 November 2011

Please sponsor David if you can spare some pennies or dirhams, poor love's got a face full of hair for a fantastic cause and of course Anna too with her half marathon! You guys rock!

16 November 2011

Not a fabulous day today although made much more bearable by the lovely Fee and Karen coming over for supper! The oncologist appointment didn't go quite to plan! After the two delays already, I am now looking at another 10-14 days before I can start the chemo because they can't fit me in! I didn't see the oncologist but his registrar, I daren't say what I really think on such a public platform, but it wasn't quite the

---

[1] Strictly Come Dancing: a dance show where celebrities are paired with professional dancers and learn a new dance every week. Very glitzy and glamorous—very Sally.

experience I had hoped for. He literally read a list of all the side effects my chemo combination would cause, including: total hair loss (the cold cap will give me about a 10 per cent chance of keeping 20 per cent of my hair), eyebrow and eyelash loss, sickness, tiredness, bad stomach, higher risk of blood clots, heart problems, skin problems, prone to infections…the list went on and on and on! I was literally just laughing because I had no idea how else to cope with it. The poor man was just doing his job, but his bedside manner was not great by any stretch! The positive in all of this is despite the aggressive nature of the chemo I am looking at it curing me of this bloody cancer…Well, there'll always be a 10 per cent chance of it returning but the odds are much better. I've just got to suck it up and see I suppose. As you know I've been so positive and this is the first time I've felt knocked down a little. A certain person dragged me back off the floor though early this evening and is a pretty amazing support at the mo, thank you! I have no doubt when I've slept on this tonight; I will feel a million times better and no doubt see the good things! Thank goodness for the wig hey!

18 November 2011

…and breathe! Feel much better today and looks like plans remain unchanged. Try the chemo here, see how it affects me, fly home in between the second and third cycle then finish in Dubai as long as I'm not puking, crapping, crawling etc…Will almost defo be bald…I'm trying to embrace this hence going on about it! Tomorrow eyebrows! I do not lie…fingers crossed I don't end up looking like a drag queen! Have been on the phone with Macmillan today and have to say they are the most helpful people ever. They literally have answered every question I've had. Well, off to Bedfordshire now…night all.

19 November 2011

News to report…Ok, I'm not going to lie…The eyebrows are quite dark! Now, apparently, they will fade by about 40 per cent over the next couple of days, but for now, they look like one of two things…A pair of slugs or comedy Christmas cracker eyebrows. I have to wear huge amounts of eye liner and mascara to compensate for this look. My dad is trying to make me feel better by telling me they are definitely fading every day—he feels bad as when he picked me up from having them done his first words were 'bloody hell mate, they're a bit dark!'

I've had some really interesting conversations with people regarding the chemo over the last couple of days. I know of three people who have had exactly the same combination of drugs as me and have been relatively fine, two of them lost their hair but one kept it. I'm still trying not to fixate on this, what will be or as my lovely friend Kate said today 'que sera sera'…Love a bit of Doris!

I'm also doing a lot of reading about diet and how to prevent cancer cell formulating. A lot of people have told me to drink plenty of water during the chemo as well! I must admit I'm not drinking nearly as much as I do in Dubai. My darling, Alan thinks drinking loads of water is hilarious as my bladder will be weak and, in his words, *you'll end up pissing yourself.* Some things will never change!

It was Kerry's birthday yesterday…Was lovely to see you all on Skype and made me miss you masses…I would have done anything to be with you all yesterday…Kerry, you were looking stunning mate, hope you had a fab day. Well…while I'm on a quoting blog day, in Bugs Bunny's famous words: 'That's All Folks!'

20 November 2011

The eyebrows are fading and I'm feeling ok out in public. Now either I've got used to the slugs and the general public is still subtly pissing themselves at my expense or they really are starting to look real! Had a lovely day yesterday with Amanda and Lizzie, lots of giggles and Reigate has become one of my new favourite places…The shops are just gorgeous…I needed a whole day and a purse full of cash, we can but dream! All topped off with a lovely evening with Amanda's sister and Mum, Strictly and X Factor! I love Little Mix and am totally over-excited to be going to see the show on Sunday! Fingers crossed that the chemo starts after this or at least that I remain relatively sick free…I don't think vomiting at the live show would go down particularly well…Vomiting over Stephen less so! Bit of JC tomorrow to assess the wounds! I've got a couple of areas where scabs have come off and left bloody areas, apparently, this is a good sign! Just hope the chemo can go ahead with these!

Am reading a fabulous book called *Anti-Cancer A New Way of Living* and am shoving the fruit, veg and green tea down me like it's going out of fashion. Also, got to get some turmeric and ginger into the diet and am going to cut out red meat, saturated fat, sugar (no more biscuits:-() and most dairy; the odd bit of organic cheese will be passing my lips I'm sure. I've also ordered a chemotherapy recipe book, but any recipes you guys have that you think would be suitable would be warmly received.

Well done to David and Anna who are doing some pretty amazing fund raising at the moment, there is going to be no stopping me when this is over and I will learn to run, even if it kills me, before September! Big hugs.

22 November 2011

Blog is here…just incredibly late. Had an appointment at the McIndoe today with JC and you'll be pleased to hear everything is in the last stages of healing and the bio-oil can now come out to help these scars reduce…What was about 15 dressings is now down to a bit of magic cream and a plaster! Love it! JC also asked me how I'd got on with the oncologist, when I told him of my plight he insisted that the oncologist was a plonker and I was to stay positive…Good man that JC, only one more session with him as then of course a whole series of minor ops next year to tidy any bits up and of course pop on a nipple…knew you were all thinking it;-).

Dubai people will be pleased to hear that JC has been in touch with Dr Coach my consultant over there, I've sent all my pathology reports and they are busy sorting a smooth transfer from the UK to Dubai with the chemo…Fingers, toes, cherubs, you name it crossed that my body copes with this ok and I can make the flight back smoothly. It feels like I've been away forever!

Had the most delightful evening with Helen, Richard and the adorable Clara, lots of giggles, Winnie the Pooh (man, that book is hard to sight read) and plenty of green tea, I'm telling you folks it's the way forward!

Pre-chemo assessment tomorrow…Going on my own to this one, brave girl that I am, it'll give me a chance to talk about cold caps and lines etc…After a lot of thought have decided to stick with the cannulas rather than having something stuck inside me 24/7 and they only offer a PICC[2] line at Guildford, look it up, it's dead interesting.

Big hugs to you all xxxx.

24 November 2011

I am a dickhead…But then we all knew that! I completely ignored a piece of paper that came with my pre-assessment appointment. First chemo session is this Friday…Oh shitty doo dar! Crapping my pants!

24 November 2011

Day before Day (first chemo)! Have had a lovely couple of days in London. Apart from falling flat on my arse out of a lift (asks Alan), it was just perfect! Thank you, Alan!! And thank you Rooney for a lovely dinner last night.

I'm going to sound very American right now (it is Thanksgiving!)…There has not been a day since the 6 September when I haven't had a text, card, email, phone call, WhatsApp, hug etc. from one of you. I am the luckiest girl (hate woman…makes me sound old!!) and I go into tomorrow knowing how much support and love I have from the most amazing people. I feel truly blessed! Thank you, people…you have no idea how bloody brilliant you all are.

So, on the train home last night I get stuck in front of an older man who coughs (like a really ill wintry cough) for 24 minutes without putting his hand over his mouth…Please

---

[2] Peripherally inserted catheter line—there are differences in length, thickness and durability but as Sally said, 'look it up, it's dead interesting'.

imagine me, panicking about the chemo and my immune system and finding myself holding my breath! Oh dear! What has my world come to?

Tomorrow I will be going early to the hospital in order to don the cold cap, half an hour before the chemo and an hour after…Brain freeze here I come. Please keep your fingers, toes, arms and legs crossed that I'm not sick…Got a date with Gary Barlow, Paul and Stephen on Sunday and I so wanna be there! Surely that face alone is worth a prescription!

Have a lovely weekend Dubai people and only one more day UK. Lots of love to you all. 25 November 2011 Cycle One finished! (It's like ANTM[3]) All ok! Persevered with the ice cap, was a bit worried for the first 20 minutes and gave me the right hump, but after that it was ok, just means I have to stay in the hospital for ages afterwards.

Met lots of people at the hospital and had some dead interesting conversations. Everyone from someone on cycle five of the treatment to a girl the same age as me who was now in palliative care…so sad, but she was dead upbeat…Well, sort of, until she told me that she had breast cancer and had the same drugs as me 'you'll be fine for the next few days then you'll feel shit!' Oh great! Am soooo looking forward to my break by the seaside! Got my anti-sickness drugs, ginger, green tea and plenty of water so fingers crossed. On steroids for a couple of days, so looks like I'll be ok for Gary :-).

My mum absolutely peed herself when I took the ice cap off, the nurse said I looked like a lolly pop! I like to think she was comparing me to Victoria Beckham…I can see the

---

[3] America's Next Top Model—pretty much what it says on the tin!

resemblance, especially with that helmet on. Now for fuzzy hair, no styling or straighteners OMG.

Dubai peeps I could do with some help…Apparently, the GICC[4] don't do cold caps, could you find out if the American Hospital do and if I could hire them? Any help from your end would be very much appreciated!

Lots of love to you all and I know I joke a bit on these blogs, but I'm still me…I am determined not to become a victim to this or lose me…I still get grumpy sometimes (first 20 minutes of cold cap was a prime Hitchcock grumpy example—imagine the face ache).

28 November 2011

Dear all, had a lovely night last night at X-Factor live and was well looked after by the lovely Stephen and Paul.

The chemo seems to be ok *touch wood.* Bar feeling decidedly ropey on Friday, I seem to be reasonably ok. I stop the anti-sickness and steroids tomorrow so fingers crossed this lasts! I have been told the tiredness might well kick in then. On the whole though, all good.

As you know I wore the ice cap on Friday. Now all the info about keeping your hair says to wash occasionally and then leave. Good plan unless you have hair like mine. So, yesterday I washed and left it…went like a hair bear so I quietly straightened it then convinced my parents that it just miraculously straightened itself! So, not cool and so going to really, really regret this if it starts falling out! I'll be honest with you, this is without doubt my biggest fear, but as I've said before I'll just have to suck it up and see!

---

[4] Gulf International Cancer Centre

I'm going to the seaside for a week today to recoup at my friend's lovely holiday home. I'm hoping a good dose of sea air and r & r will do me the world of good. I won't have Internet access a lot of the time though so I'm afraid the blogs might be few and far between…Enjoy the rest of me harping on folks;-).

Sending big hugs to you all, all over the world.

29 November 2011

What a fabulous night! Thank you, lovely Stephen and Paul!

4 December 2011

Have just come back from the loveliest, loveliest time in my friend's house by the seaside. Lovely walks on the beach, breakfasts in a beautiful cafe overlooking the sea, wonderful food (must admit I didn't do a lot of the cooking) and great company. I feel totally spoilt, refreshed and relaxed. I'm telling you this should be on prescription after chemo. Finished the tablets on Monday and not at all sick, little tired at times, but still managed to walk about a mile a day and just slowed down when needed. I know this doesn't sound a lot, but I have just unpacked my bags this evening and am totally knackered…ridiculous! I now have to write a reference…so should have done that in the week, some things never change :-).

Andrew and David Knotts have raised an absolute fortune for 'Breast Cancer Care' while I've been away which is just! Well done boys and thank you to all of you who donated; this is really something I want to do more of when I'm better…I'll be looking for training from the Hamster, Sarah Hamm, to get me back to full fitness and then the fundraising can begin. I need to talk to the oncologist and sort out my transfer…I'm intending to fly back on the 29th/30th December. I worked out today with a friend that this is only three and a half weeks away! I can't believe the time has gone so fast and that I'll be back in Dubai. I'm really looking forward to some normality back in my life, but at the same time am a little scared…what if the treatment is different? What if they give me different anti-sickness drugs? What if I get stressed at work? What if I'm sick? Anyway, I'm sure you can imagine! Like everything, I'll just have to suck it up and see. I am looking forward to seeing everyone though and can't tell you how much you're missed Dubai family! I also can't wait to get back to the kids and get my IGCSE group back, it's been driving me mad not knowing what they're up to, especially as they're the brightest bunch of students I have ever taught! Not really helped by an email from the kids telling me they've not been as focused!

Right, enough of my ramblings…Thank you, Helen Brimblecombe, for letting us stay in your gorgeous house and to Neil Broughton for putting up with me for a whole week…not easy and very well managed, even if I did lose every argument! And Jonathan Blake and Stephen for feeding the cancer with a great big sugary cake! Shit! Better get back to the anti-cancer recipes this week!

Oh and one more thing…I still have hair!

6 December 2011

Today I have had confirmation of my treatment in Dubai. Seeing the oncologist on the 3rd Jan and then the first chemo on Sunday, 8 January! All good! There is one distressing part, the GICC have told me that I can't wear a cold cap which means folks, and I'm going to lose my hair. This has upset me more than anything else I've had to deal with in this whole process and in some respects my vanity has saved me on so many levels—slightly bizarre from someone who wouldn't have considered themselves vain before now.

I'm now faced with two challenges, do I wear the cold cap next week and try to keep my hair for Christmas and then just embrace the baldness with the New Year, or do I accept it now? I think the first one perhaps...who knows? What worries me the most is looking sick...I'm really scared that this will make me feel so much worse than I need to. I suppose I've just got to suck it up and see and bloody get on with it!

This morning I've been working and the saddo in me was happy being back at it. Now to find flights home which are proving difficult and really bloody expensive.

Big hugs everyone...onwards and upwards!

6 December 2011

Ulcers...A chemo side effect! Nuff said! Oh, and achy boob again, chemo should have stopped my periods—am awaiting another Hitchcock miracle...it's that box of luck people, I'm telling you! And if you have any good cures for ulcers please send them my way...was going to say something awful then but have stopped myself!

8 December 2011

Today is a sad day...My last appointment with JC who I might add loves me—I'm sure of it! Well until the nipple reconstruction that is! He's asked me to be a spokesperson over in Dubai for reconstructive surgery so people coming over to the UK for the op can come talk to me first. I also might do some vids for him in the future (clean minds please) and he's coming over to the desert end of March/beginning of April for the first-ever breast conference in the UAE! This is fabulous and really means that the UAE is working hard to keep up to date with all the breast cancer developments. Soooo, all good and more importantly I'm healing like a good girl :-). I went and said hello to all the nurses at the McIndoe and they were like 'oh, my god…have you not started chemo…you look fab!'

One nurse said I looked like I'd put on a bit of weight :-(Not so good and I totally blame Neil Broughton for cooking me far too much lovely food last week. My dad thought the comment was hilarious and then decided to keep on about me putting weight on! Bloody charming, especially as I've just had to buy clothes a size smaller! I can only think I must have been well skinny for a while there! Needless to say, it's the only healthy option today—do I sound paranoid? 1 a.m.!

So, now to tell the oncologist here I'm returning to Dubai and booking my flight back with Rhian…she's going to let me know if my wig slips! I'm relying on you all when I'm back…don't go enjoying my unfortunateness!

One other lovely, lovely thing today…my friend Saz (you all know her as Sarah in Hawaii soon to be Bahrain) has written me a song which I love and know you will too. I'm going to try and copy and paste it on to here so you can listen, it will make you chuckle…I think Sarah knows me far too well, thank you for that Mrs! Do we want a copy of the lyrics?

Today I am mostly knackered! Well, they did say the tiredness would come and it hit me like a tonne of bricks this afternoon so it's a snooze for me. Off to Chi tomorrow and then Sunday roast dinner and Christmas tree decorating with my gorgeous godson…Can't wait!

Have a lovely weekend Dubai peeps and see you soon…hopefully in London town! The rest of you, get back to it! You've got another 27 hours till your weekend;-).

12 December 2011

First clump of hair in my hands! Mel's words 'That's quite a lot'. Oh shitty doo dah! Will be phoning up my amazing hairdresser John this week then…sad times!

13 December 2011

I think it's fair to say that what started as a lovely day seems to have gone downhill. My fricking hair is falling out…it is bloody everywhere and getting on everybody; I have a bloody cold; I have my blood tomorrow and have just had to send a shitty work email. I think we can safely say I am going to bed one pissed off and fed up lady. Bloody hope tomorrow is better I'm telling you gggrrrrrrrrrrr! There is a funny story involving a phone call, but I haven't even got the energy to share that one :-(.

14 December 2011

Am biting the bullet and having all my hair cut off tomorrow! Figure I've got to go with it. Good job I have a lovely hairdresser and friend who will put up with my tears!;-). Red wig is getting the chop and a new blonde one is as well.

The oncologist appointment went well and it's all confirmed folks…I'm flying back to the desert on the 29 December! I am soooo going to miss my UK family and friends but hopefully lots of visits over the coming months.

Fingers crossed the cold hasn't completely mucked up the bloods and the chemo will go ahead as planned on Friday…Just want it all over and done with and after Friday a third will be done :-).

Sorry about my moans yesterday folks, much better day today and smiling! The hair is still an issue, especially in this weather when it is literally blowing out in the wind FFS, no one warned me about this! At least short hair will cause less mess! Am still devastated this is happening but this was the bit I dreaded so just got to get on with it and someone reminded me it's only going to happen once!

Big hugs and lots of love from a happier lady than yesterday!

Ok…this is probably about the 10th clump to come out today…I don't want you to think I'm exaggerating this! Shit shit bloody shit! Poor John, how the hell is he going to cut it, they'll be more on the comb! This is not going to get me down…Aaaarrrrgggghhh! Sharing is caring and all that!

16 December 2011

Am hoping this might last till Christmas! John Mullan is a brave man…there was hair everywhere!!! Well, here are the halfway mark folks!

Getting fired up…Feeling like Audley Harrison Ding a ling a ling, round two here we come! Could be a quick process if I don't wear the ice cap…Bloody hair is coming out by the hour; I have a huge bald patch on the top of my head—attractive! Not great when you realise you have less hair than your dad and your mum (who I might add is thinning these days). Got to get through this week and get used to the wigs and cover-ups and then I'm sure I'll be on the up again. It's my own fault for dreading this the most!!! Got myself a lovely cheeky scarf in M&S (they've got a designer Walender doing pieces for them)…Might have to purchase another and look at a couple more wigs. If I'm going to rock this, we're going to have some fun…You will not know what is going on in the Foremarke Office[5], red, blonde, long, short!

No point trying to pretend it's real when it's clearly not! Off to Bedfordshire now, got a cough so not sleeping great, but have given myself the next three days to get over the second round of chemo, then away again for another recoup!

Night peeps…sleep tight.

18 December 2011

It's official…I am now sporting a French crop! That's bald to you and I have had the shittest couple of days while it's been falling out, so Wendy's husband Lorenzo shaved it all off for me this afternoon. I have to say, I feel a bit relieved it's over…this has by far been the hardest thing I've had to deal with. It's done now and actually; I don't look as awful as I thought I might! Bloody cold head though, going to have to wear a woolly hat to bed tonight.

19 December 2011

Got a hole in my boob…I kid you not! Think I have done the right thing and dressed well (becoming an expert) but need to phone the hospital to see what they think! Bummer! And due to the chemo, everything is not healing at the pace it was! Am supposed to be going away on Tues night to Sandbanks

---

[5] The school had several Houses. Sally was Head of house for Foremark.

for some r&r, walks on the beach and lovely food so have my fingers crossed I'll be able to!

Am slowly getting used to the bald head, but am a little surprised every time I cop a look in the mirror. Considering it was the thing I was most scared of I think I've embraced it as much as I can.

My dearest Lizzie (aka my lil sis) flew in from New Zealand yesterday…It's so lovely to have her back and she's flying out to Dubai with me for a week before she embarks on more exciting travels. I think the baldness was a bit of a shock, but the wigs will be making their first public appearance today so we shall see!

I have never felt so unorganised for Christmas and I send apologies for the lack of cards, but sending loads of Christmas love and cheer to you all.

21 December 2011

Hole sorted! Big kiss from JC and we're going for a drink when he comes to Dubai in April…his suggestion! He's only human :-).

Anyway, have got to learn not to tell everyone I meet I'm wearing a wig! My fav tag line at the mo is 'I've lost all my hair—got a wig on!' When will I learn to keep it shut? Was sure everyone in the world could tell, but who knows? The wig has had its first outing…I went for the TOWIE look! It's taking another trip to the cinema tonight and then to London tomorrow!! I think I will name my TOWIE wig JC after the man himself! Soooo, I have a reddy brown one to name and hopefully will have purchased a human hair one tomorrow! This is going to cost me more than my Chloe bag, you girls will know this brings a tear to my eye, but needs must and am figuring it might be a bit cooler on the head in Dubai.

Suggestions for the naming of the other two please people...it's sounding a bit like a dog on my head!

Am far more positive now the hair is gone, unbelievable considering last week I felt like I hit a real low, as you all know the hair was an issue!

I'm off tomorrow for a few days by the seaside for some more post-chemo rest and relaxation and a good dose of fresh air so may not be able to blog.

Love you all and I seriously thank you all every day from the bottom of my heart for your continuous support and kind words that get me through each day.

24 December 2011

Have just had the loveliest few days away at Sandbanks. Been looked after, visited some lovely friends, was cooked for and generally had some great r & r by the seaside. I had no idea how beautiful the beaches were down there...even in December! And today's been topped off with a visit from Jo Taylor who's home for Christmas! Lovely times. You see, in the worst times good things happen and as I say all the time 'everything happens for a reason!' I am still very conscious of the wigs, but I think the red is more realistic so figuring I'm going to have to go for that most of the time. I got complimented on my film star smile and eyes in the pub this evening! Ok, he was old, blind and deaf but WTF! I told him to join the queue!

I usually love Christmas as you all know, I come home every year without fail, but this is perhaps the weirdest one yet, possibly worse than my first Christmas back as a singleton after my hideous split! I think seeing everyone's good cheer, happy faces, and excitement and dare I say it…Champagne! It sometimes hits me a little like a ramrod and I find myself thinking 'shit…I've got cancer!' I then get a Hitchcock grip and remind myself that this is a temporary hiccup, pull myself together and get on with it. I am looking forward to spending Christmas with lovely family and friends and think maybe the gremlin in me is just a little pissed off that the one glass of champagne will have to suffice this year…bugger it, I'll make up for it next year!

Night all and a Happy Christmas Eve. Remember if you're feeling down, there's another one next year so you may as well just get on and enjoy it :-).

24 December 2011

The Hitch is back…thought I best post this in case you don't recognise me next week folks!

27 December 2011

What a whirlwind a couple of days. A lovely Christmas Day with the Petries…drank far too much and had to stop when my pee turned funny! Whoops! A lovely Boxing Day with the family with a long dog walk all around the old A3…amazing the landscaping they've done already to bring the punchbowl's former glory back. And then another long dog walk with Wendy and Kerry today followed by lots of visitors, cups of tea and biscuits topped off with a good old English pub tea with Miss Coburn all the way from Dubai. Happy as a pig in shit:-). Now to begin the mammoth task of packing! Oh goodness, where to start? I'm coming home to Dubai peeps…although feeling absolutely distraught about leaving all my family and friends over here at the same time. I will defo keep my blog going though it's just going to be the other way round if that makes sense. Boo and hooray have never seemed appropriate in the same sentence (well unless you're at panto) but that best sums up what's going on right now. Hope you've all had a lovely jubbly Christmas and all your dreams come true in 2012.

27 December 2011

Little sis Lizzie changing her plans and staying till the 17th yipeeeeeeee! She gets to come on the chemo run :-). And look after me!

29 December 2011

Flight is sorted, so I suppose this will be my last post in the UK :-(Very sad to be leaving everyone…I could not have gotten through the last three months without you all popping in, taking me for days out, weeks away, trips to the cinema, weekends in Chi, visits to the hospital and making my room the party room…you name it! I am going to miss you all sooo much, but know I'm going to be well cared for and looked after by my Dubai family and friends.

I cannot wait to be in my flat, in my own bed and feel a little more in control of my life. I'll keep you all updated…no more JC but Rich Blanc and Dr Mulberry! I'm sure I'll have some nicknames for them before you know it. Wonder if they're prepared for the return of me…bet they don't know what they've let themselves in for. Am hoping that the cultural difference doesn't frighten me too much, but as I say I have loads of support! Lizzie is over for chemo 3, Mum and

Dad for chemo 4 and maybe Neil for chemo 5 plus the girls and boys who make up my Dubai family!

I am one lucky girl to have you all in my life and feel really lucky to have been given the opportunity to appreciate you all (does that sound a bit wanky?—fuck it! Sorry, Mum). So, see you soon Dubai peeps and thank you dear UK people for being so wonderful while I've been home. Now if only I could have you all in the same country at the same time.

1 January 2012

Happy New Year lovely people and a big thank you for all your support, love and encouragement in 2011! 2012 will have an interesting start to it, four chemos and what sounds like shed loads of radiotherapy, but everything crossed for a healthy one.

It's lovely being back in Dubai although I'm providing a few shocks with the wigs etc. and having to go through the reveal of the baldie head. Can't even begin to tell you how lovely it is to be back in my flat and sleeping like a baby in my own bed!

New Year's resolutions will include lots of organic food, a healthy anti-cancer diet (most of the time), a new juicer and exercise—don't worry Mrs Partridge I will check in with you on that one. I also have a few others that I won't bore you with. In the most bizarre way, I'm quite looking forward to 2012!

Jamie's Italian for me tonight with Lizzie, Sam and Dawn, really looking forward to it and the fireworks :-).

To all my friends, enjoy Yalumba, Cold Play, Titanic in Brixton, Chichester, Bournemouth, Philly (guessing that's where you are, Saz), Washington, beach parties, anywhere you're spending it, you name it! Miss you UK people more than I can tell you and Dubai people I'm so looking forward to catching up with you all properly. It's good to be back!

Much love, health and fortune to you all for 2012.

2 January 2012

Back to work tomorrow! Went in today and am a little nervous to say the least-especially with the wiggage! Hugs are good, but must remember the toupee tape so it doesn't keep sliding off…I kid you not! I must also remember not to get stressed! My body has developed a new way of telling me that I need to stop—I start swelling at the side of the reconstructed booby and then can't put my arm down fully. Get me with my newfound ailments!

Had a little bit of a homesick moment last night when I came off Skype :-(. You know what it's like; you get used to being home. I won't deny the fact that I have well and truly missed my bed though. Had a fab NY with Dawn, Sam and Lizzie and managed to gain a TV and a pair of clippers!! I have some good mates I'm telling you, then a lovely breakfast at Jones' on New Year's Day. Had overdone it a little so came home, had a good sleep and chilled on the sofa like a good girl. Do not worry, Mum, they are watching me like a hawk over here! School, breast surgeon and oncologist tomorrow so a busy day, but good to get everything sorted before round 3 on Sunday. Everyone says I look well and my boobs still look big! They are four sizes smaller people—I must be standing up tall.

3 January 2012

Goodbye, ice cap…welcomes baldness! The decision was made; didn't wear the cold cap as the bald patch on the top of my head is quite extreme now! Mum is a bit pissed off that I said her hair was thinning…whoops!!

Well, cycle two (the last chemo in the UK) is now over! Onwards and upwards. I am about to embrace wigs, hats and even scarves (sorry Michael) but I bloody intend to still look glam if it kills me!

Young girl next to me today on her first chemo; she must have been in her twenties, that's when you realise life is unfair at times. You'll be pleased to know I gave her lots of good advice about wigs, eyebrows and anti-sickness! In all fairness, she was probably glad when I stopped talking!

Now going to lie on the sofa and watch crap TV with my fingers crossed the anti-sickness drugs work their magic.

6 January 2012

Sitting in the hospital waiting for blood and waiting for insurance approval! Same shit, different country! There are days when you wonder how anyone is cured of anything! You got to laugh, unbelievable!

6 January 2012

What an interesting day! School was totally overwhelming this morning and I think the kids are having a few issues with the wiggage! Will reveal the baldness if they're not careful. Think they are just a little shocked I'm back and have no idea how to cope, poor things. Not every day you have a teacher with cancer hey! Then went to the breast surgeon who seemed to have fallen out with the breast nurse and the hospital so that was a bit awkward. This was followed by the bloody long drive to the Gulf International Cancer Centre where the oncologist (nice guy) has found a flaw with my notes! Dubai findings show triple positive breast cancer, UK say triple-negative—so this needs looking into. I've always known I was awkward, but this is bloody ridiculous! It of course has a knock-on effect on the treatment I will be given. Sunday I will continue as normal but if they find it is positive, I will have to have Herceptin introduced to the treatment...for a year! The good side of this is if it is positive, the success rate is greater so a double-edged sword and one I can't worry about until they sort the findings. Oncologist in Dubai is now in touch with a breast surgeon in the UK. After all of this, I then got home and managed to wax the hair off at the front of my head (only a bit left) with the toupee tape! Not a great day, but still smiling, despite getting very little sleep last night and working myself up into a frenzy at 3 a.m. this morning! Thank god for Alan Bradshaw!

So, back to school properly tomorrow and sitting tight to await the findings as to who has made a mistake with my notes...can you Adam and Eve it?

Keep smiling, Sally! Don't get stressed, rest and walk tall—and don't talk about yourself in the third person, very sad;-).

8 January 2012

Lamb to the Slaughter Part 3! Here's hoping a) they find a vein and b) they do anti-sickness well in the Middle East! To say I'm shitting myself is, my friends, an understatement!! I am absolutely petrified! Fingers crossed it's as plain sailing as it was in the UK. At the end of today, I'll be at the halfway mark! Yey!

8 January 2012

Later that day: No veins so no chemo! Now at City Hospital in the VIP room waiting for a small op to have a portocath fitted! I am telling you now people are thankful you are not me or Evelyn right now for that matter!

9 January 2012

Have had op this afternoon where they have inserted a portocath into my chest! This will mean they will be able to administer the chemo without the veins. Bit uncomfortable tonight, but that's because they have a needle secured to me ready for tomorrow and the incision is a little sore! At least it's done now so back to the GICC for the chemo tomorrow. What a day! Thank you, Evelyn, for driving, making me smile and looking after me today. Two thousand pounds lighter in the pocket so here's hoping the insurance approves this tomorrow and I get my refund. Who said Dubai was a breeze? Lots of love to you all.

10 January 2012

Cycle three of the chemo, done and dusted! I am now halfway through, peeps! Fingers crossed for the anti-nausea drugs working their magic! It looks like the radiotherapy will run into Easter so as much as I am gagging to get back to the UK it's looking unlikely :-(.

11 January 2012

Stayed at home this morning; this was very much needed. Then to school for a full-on afternoon followed by parents' evening! I am whacked! Went through all of my meds with the school doc so now happy to take them! The anti-sickness seems to be working their magic so that's a huge relief. I also managed to administer my injection :-). Have five days of these to boost my immune system and I won't deny I was petrified, but at the end of the day, thinking I'd gone through four ops in fewer months, three lots of chemo and sitting with a friend whose kids inject themselves every day because of their type 1 diabetes, I thought 'come on, Pitchfork, you can bloody well do this!' and bloody well do this I did. I am well proud of myself; the needle's a proper two-inch one and everything!

Well another day over, the confusion between triple-negative and triple-positive continues. I am inclined to believe that the UK are right although the result is not the best of the two…we will have to pay for the privilege of another test and of course more money! It's not cheap getting cancer, kids!

I have a new wig on its way to the folks, a blonde bob this time. This week I am donning the blonde TOWIE wig which seems to be a hit with the kids…so much so that two came to find me today to tell me they prefer this one to the reddy bob. My friend and I have decided the red bob makes me look like Velma from Scooby-Doo! Here's hoping someone has a fancy dress soon!

Right enough nattering, bed for me it's late and you all keep telling me I need my rest. Sleep tight, people.

13 January 2012

Injection done—all by myself! Jeesh I never thought I'd have it in me! Call from docs last night to say definitely triple-negative! Not great to have had the false hope but at least we know where we are! Nurse Lizzie is looking after me, making me lots of ginger tea and a few lessons have been learnt this week! I definitely need to take it easy and put my health first!!

Had a lovely evening last night, dinner with Lizzie and good company at Adele and Andy's…just what the doctor ordered followed by a very, very long sleep! Thanks, everyone for keeping me going this week…it's been a hard one!

14 January 2012

Looking attractive in the hospital yesterday! Anyone wants to swap lives right now—offers welcome!

17 January 2012

You just couldn't write a book about my life right now, I'm telling you! Have just had a call from my breast consultant—JC's mate—to tell me the pathologist in Dubai read my results as triple-negative, however, in the transcript it got written down as triple positive! Thank the bloody lord that I had my first lot of treatment in the UK…goodness knows what mistakes would have been made on me! I now have to write a letter of complaint. This has effectively resulted in every patient in the last two years under my consultant having to be retested to check their results are correct! Would you Adam and Eve it! I cannot begin to tell you how this worries me about my treatment here, although my breast consultant will be keeping a close eye on everything that goes on, I think JC will kill him otherwise—I'm precious cargo you know! Having a pedicure and reflexology now to help me de-stress…Lizzie's last night here :-(. Next out mum and dad a week today…watch out Dubai else Rottweiler Hitchcock aka Mum will be after you!;-). Be good and stay healthy!

21 January 2012

Awkward moment at the gym…"Miss Sally, you have been for long time."

Me: "Yes I've not been well."

Manager: "Oh yes, what's been wrong with you?"

Me: "Breast cancer."

Him: "Oh no…That's bad!"

No shit, mate! Plus side, a few more prayers in my favour!

22 January 2012

I can only write this here…too much cake—cancer feeder! Oh shit! Tasted good though and it is my birthday! Am seriously hoping the cancer isn't hungry today!

29 January 2012

Chemo 4 done and surprisingly feel ok, just tired! Fell asleep having the chemo today so an instant effect. I am now two-thirds through :-). The end is in sight!

Radiotherapy will hopefully start three weeks after 11 March. Evelyn and I are putting a rota together as the daily trip to Abu Dhabi could prove a little exhausting. I hate to ask but lots of you have asked how can you help, if you fancy doing a trip with me let me know when's good and we'll add you. Trying desperately to sort it around my teaching timetable, especially the IGCSE class. Let me know folks it'll be Sunday to Thursday for six weeks so one trip would make all the difference.

30 January 2012

Chemo four and the drug change! Bloody nerves have woken me up at a God-awful hour this morning. Took my steroids last night as this one is quite strong so you have to take steroids before and after the chemo. Read the side effects and one of them is 'moon face'. I ask you…'moon face!' But I already have a moon face…what the hell's mine going to look like if it gets any more moony? Bald and moony! Omg!

Blood this weekend was eventually taken from my hand, my veins have totally had enough of this and for someone who was never needle-phobic, it is becoming a problem. Really looking forward to another five days of self-injecting as well. Actually, I do feel ever so proud of myself each day I do it. Sometimes I wonder how I get through each day and if a little bit of me thinks I'm playing a role…'do not forget this experience' my old voice teacher would say, well I tell you…thanks, Joe; this is one experience I won't forget in a hurry.

People keep telling me I'm 'brave' and 'inspirational' at the moment…these words are the highest compliment…I'm not brave or inspirational, I feel humble that people would use those words in a sentence with my name. I'm just getting on and bloody determined not to let this get me down. Maybe the fact that work is providing me with plenty of distractions is a good thing…Stops me dwelling too much on myself, although I think I am in danger of becoming a cancer bore—please slap me appropriately at any point, but mind the moon face.

Right, another hour of sleep, please. Thank you, lovely people, without sounding totally American…thank you for seeing me through the days at the moment and people at school, I could not have gotten through some of the last couple of weeks without you—bloody hell…you couldn't write a book could you—well only if your name was SJ…dim-witted indeed!

30 January 2012

In all honesty, I am not an attractive prospect this morning! Face like a beetroot from the steroids! Alan Bradshaw, I know you are now pissing yourself laughing! Bald and red!

Mum is currently washing the TOWIE wig so fingers crossed it doesn't shrink in the process…oh what I'd give for my normal life back right now. Plenty of rest today in the hope I feel back to full health tomorrow ready for the House Shout[6]! Well, the good thing is at least my face is the right colour for Foremarke House…got to look at the positives folks!

31 January 2012

So two days ago, chemo four done and dusted…I repeat that means only two more to go! The end is in sight :-). Going to discuss radiotherapy on 19 February and as long as no complications this will start three weeks after 11 March. I'm going to sit with Ev and work out a radiotherapy rota…six weeks of Sunday to Thursday everyday…will be tiring on my

---

[6] In the 'House Shout' each House would select a song to sing as a House in competition with other Houses. Good fun and highly competitive!

own so if you fancy being put on the rota let me know when is good. Surprisingly feel ok, just tired…Fell asleep when I had the chemo today, sort of knocked me for six! So, good to know I only have a third left though :-) xxx

4 February 2012

Off work today with the most awful pains in my legs and feet…went to the bathroom in the night and practically had to crawl there. Will phone the hospital this morning as it might just be that I need to rest. There is no doubt that being back in Dubai has definitely taken its toll at times and there has been a lot of stress. Well let's hope the legs get sorted…being stuck in bed is not a great prospect. Billy Ocean is on tonight as well—not really want to do a Little Britain's Andy to that one…Adele and Bradders, you could be taking your 'special' friend out!

4 February 2012

Later: Just had the most fab evening at Billy Ocean…Most human I have felt since coming back and totally forgot about all the crap going on…Only prob, ducking and diving to miss-pissed people dancing with fags in their hands…I'm highly flammable right now! Thank you so much, Adele and Andy! I am now going to bed singing Billy Ocean with a great big fat grin on my face…'When the going gets tough…' Night all.

10 February 2012

You know I'm back working as I don't have nearly enough time to update this—sorry, folks. The horrible effects from the last dose of chemo are slowly wearing off and I'm feeling far more human and have much more energy this week which is lovely! I have also upped the five a day to eight a day and this is helping too—we are what we eat! Damn that doughnut today! Funny things this week—there's a rumour going around the younger ones that my hair has grown back, but I just like wearing a wig! Lovely, year 8 boy said, "That wig looks like your own hair Miss, but when you get nearer you can see it's plastic!" Plastic…cheeky little thing! Today I went to a year 12 biology class…they gave me a presentation on cancer cells and then I shared my story with them, even showed them the bald head. It was a really humbling experience and if any good can come from this bloody disease then I'm a happier lady. The kids were so sensitive with their questions and very very sweet. If it helps one of them with their studies or helps them realise that cancer is not a word, we can't say then fab! Break up for half-term tomorrow and I can't wait! Good night, folks.

11 February 2012

This is the time for updates…when your bloody body clock wakes you up at ridiculous o'clock during half-term! Eyebrows have now decided to thin and eyelashes are coming out rapidly meaning I am starting to resemble an albino mole—I kid you not! This is not a look I'd choose for myself and is making it increasingly difficult to look normal even with a wig and make-up! Four weeks people, four weeks, well seven at the most if you count three weeks of recovery for cycle six and the hair should start growing again…I cannot wait! As much as I love the wigs and they make getting ready in the morning so much easier I really, really, really want my own hair back now. Saw a fabulous picture of Cynthia Nixon yesterday who has shaved her hair off for a role she is playing (cancer patient). What a bitch, that's my role surely! No seriously though, she was interviewed and said she always wanted to see what she looked like with a bald head, I can understand that, it's a novelty. It's one that's wearing very thin now though! Just worked out how to do the cap lock on my iPhone…cool!

The good thing about half-term is I'm getting plenty of well-needed rest. Have got to go to school and do a bit of work as going back to inspection and chemo week—joy of joys, it's bad enough getting through the week after chemo without the added pressure of inspection too.

Very girly day for me today…lunch and nails—lovely. Have a good day everyone and enjoy your half-term teacher, people, and the rest of you…it's the weekend!

17 February 2012

Today will be the first time I have worn a wig to a wedding! Well, there you go! I will mostly be taping it down because it's a little windy over here at the mo and can you imagine if it flew off during Anna's ceremony? I will also be wearing false eyelashes as there's hardly any left. So without choice, I am becoming a Dubai girl! False tits, false hair, false eyelashes topped off with fake tan!!! Get me;-). Very excited to see Bongo looking glam in her wedding dress and looking forward to a day with great friends. Then picking another great friend up from the airport after the wedding…very very excited! I've been busy beavering away trying to get on top of work so I can enjoy the rest of the holidays, get the blood tests out of the way Friday morning then relax till Sun. Only two more of the chemos…bring it on! Nervous as hell for this one as with each one I'm feeling a little worse for wear! Seeing the radiographer as well on Sunday so will have some idea of the radiotherapy. Apparently, cold cabbage leaves in my bra are the way forward with this one, so if I pass you and you think I've farted it's the cold cabbage leaves ok;-). The right time to get up and get tidying. Lots of love everyone and happy wedding day Anna.

19 February 2012

Buggerations! Only lying awake with a stinking cold on chemo five mornings! Not sure how today's going to play out, but will let you know. Had blood yesterday so hopefully, it's just a cold and all will go ahead as scheduled, don't want to prolong this if I can help it. Have had the loveliest half-term. Having Neil over is fab, he keeps me on my toes with his rudeness and doesn't let me feel too sorry for myself! I feel very blessed that this old friend popped back into my life at such a shit time. After another failed blood test attempt on Friday, I got up to a huge gutbuster breakfast yesterday, ate a cereal bar on the way to the hospital too and drank plenty of water and the blood flowed yesterday! Hooray! These blood tests are quite frankly doing my head in! And if they tell me I'm not eating enough again I'll go mad…if anything I'm eating too much!

I had my first taste of international cricket yesterday at the Pakistan-England game and…Bloody loved it! Have a feeling this won't be the last match I go and see and now I actually understand the game it's even better! My favourite move is the four, although I'm not sure the umpire would admire my jazz hands version of it quite as much as I do. Went to Jools Holland on Friday night and Ruby Turner sang with him, fab,

fab gig and busted out some moves with the Broughton. I'm telling you now, dancing with a wig is bloody hot! And a little precarious when someone is swinging you under their arm…could have been an interesting night if I didn't have the toupee tape on!

Right…going to try and get another hour's runny-nose sleep in if I can manage it. Inspection this week at school! Can you believe it! Will keep you up to date on the chemo situation later today. Only read if interested though…I am becoming a cancer bore! UK peeps, enjoy the last day of your half-term.

20 February 2012

The radiotherapy wall chart is up and running :-), thanks everyone, so far.

Ok, Dubai folks…radiotherapy dates are now sorted…starting 25 March until 1 May, Sunday— Wednesday, 10.30 app, and Thursday 1.30 app. Had to try and best fit around my timetable at school. There are going to be two side effects to this one a burnt boob (well burnt fake boob!) and tiredness. Any help at all with these trips would be so much appreciated. The hospital has recommended I try not to drive on my own to these appointments because of the tiredness. I'm going to put a chart together today and if you can help at all I'll owe you big time. There are also a group of parents who are going to help out during school time which is really sweet of them. If anyone can help me during the Easter holidays, that would be fab! It's going to be a long six and a half weeks but the quicker I get it started the quicker I get back to full health :-). If you can help and have any preferences, let me know and I'll pop you on the chart. Thanks so much, everyone…I could not get through this without you all. I am one lucky chick I tell you to have the most fabulous friends in the world. There's a lovely poem called the 'Poorest Rich Man in the Valley', I feel like him right now, I might not have my health back yet, but I sure am enriched with fabulous, fabulous friends and really do appreciate how lucky I am.

21 February 2012

Cycle 5 done! One more to go, people, one more and then 28 days of radiotherapy starting 25 March. Guess what…I'm doing this Easter! Bugger this ruining my Easter hey! But hey, kick arse and get back to normal and if I'm really lucky JC will take me out for a drink when he comes visiting Dubai! A lovely mutton tagine cooking nicely for me this evening, I'm a lucky girl! One more…Nearly as exciting: Peterson scoring the 100 :-).

22 February 2012

Feeling a little sorry for myself today…eyebrows and eyelashes are disappearing, my taste buds are up the creek, dry as a (fill in the blanks), cracked hands and generally feel like a big albino mole! My head looks like a cress box gone wrong! I kid you not this bloody chemo malarky is not fun some days! Right, off out to dinner tonight to Pierchic, one of Dubai's finest so false eyelashes, eyebrow pencil, wig…here I come!

26 February 2012

Well, I'm not going to deny it; the last few days have been pretty tough going! Hormones all over the shot and generally have felt like absolute shit! Thank god for fabulous friends who have kept me going and told me that crying ridiculously for hours on end is perfectly acceptable! It took me every little bit of strength I had to get my sorry arse into work today, but am glad of it. It is days like this when a bit of normality is exactly what is required. For the first time yesterday, I properly felt that I just wasn't able to cope with all this; I thought I was strong and perhaps was a little complacent about what was really in store for me. So, after a hard day at school, which I managed, I felt unbelievably proud of myself, came home, slept for a few hours and then spent a lovely evening at the cricket.

Things to make you laugh...the steroid moonfaced is here...bugger that I had a moonfaced before this, it's now getting rounder and fatter by the minute! Oh well, hopefully, it'll shrink again back to normal moonfaced size!

Right, bedtime for me and a well-deserved lie-in, in the morning. Night lovely family and friends and thank you for keeping me going!

11 March 2012

I tell you now...everything in life happens for a reason and maybe, just maybe this was sent to prove a point. I have the best friends and family in the world—Fact! Yes, life has been a bit difficult over the past few years but my goodness I will not be moaning any more. My life is filled and blessed with fabulous people who hold my hand on a daily basis. Bloody hell I'm lucky. Sorry for sounding like an all-American girl but it just had to be said—thank you! Last chemo tomorrow—I cannot believe it is here! At the first one, I was most concerned with getting to X-Factor! And I made it :-). This one...well I'm just going to be concerned with getting it out of my system and getting my body back to some kind of normality! Bring it on!

12 March 2012

They can stick needles in you and pump you full of poison yet you remain positive…but put you in a machine and leave the room and you think your world is about to end! What the hell!

Last chemo done! Thank god! Had CT scan today so they could map the area for radiotherapy and then three tattoos! I now have five tattoos, two eyebrows and three dots on my boob—none are glamorous! Don't read this, Mum…I think I might have to have a tattoo!

Am staying at Evelyn's tonight and have had the loveliest evening, vegetable soup and my favourite soya yoghurts and the kids have had me in absolute stitches! Topped with major cuddles with Marley the dog! Perfect!

Fingers crossed that I don't feel as crap with this one as with the last one. Rest day tomorrow and big fat red moon face day! I am sooo looking forward to no more steroids I tell you! Now need to shift some of this water retention and weight gain and get my fat arse down the gym! I can't even begin to tell you the relief I feel that the chemo is over!

Two huge things…Paul Jones is running the London marathon in aid of prostate and breast cancer…Two charities are very very close to my heart and Steve Fantom is running the Singapore half marathon for breast cancer and another charity is extremely close to Katie and his heart, one that has touched us all! I am trying to link these to my page without much success at the mo. Please visit their pages and sponsor these two absolutely amazing men if you can.

I'm lucky…I'm living to tell my story, there are people reading this who have lost loved ones to this horrid disease…Cancer is the most individual disease that is about, every single body reacts differently, hence the research is so hard and the charities need all the help they can get! Your support might save someone.

13 March 2012

Big fat red moon face, dodgy stomach, one eyelash left on the right eye, mouth tastes like shit, sluggish and misery guts but guess what…no more chemo! Get me through this week and then I'm on the up. I will be able to go to the gym and shift some of this bloody chemo weight, hopefully, my hair, eyebrows and eyelashes will make a welcome appearance and bar looking decidedly dodgy with a short haircut for a few months…Sally-Ann Hitchcock will be back! Bring it on! Radiotherapy…brings that on too. Healthy lifestyle here I come, I am about to grab this by the horns and see the back of it! Just needed you all to know that! Lots of love.

15 March 2012

Well, that taught me! You all thought I was doing this in style! You would not have said that last night while I was bent over the loo puking, holding my banging head and wondering what the hell was going on! Unusually for me couldn't even eat anything…Well, the evening is over and after much rest today, despite being a bit wobbly on the legs I've come out the other end. And I thought chemo was going to be easy, well at least it waited until the last one before properly giving me a taste of it. Have been taking injections to boost my immune system, am sure I told you about them and I'm sure these have reacted with my body. You would have laughed had you seen me with my thermometer in my mouth while gagging. I have been told that if my temp goes to 38 degrees I have to go to the hospital—it was fine, only 36.3 So then I knew I couldn't complain too much, just had to get through the night. There was a bit of help on Skype from Alan and Katie…much appreciated and thank God the video link wasn't working…not a pretty sight!

Well, today the red moon face is starting to go down and I am pleased to say…no more steroids! Right, enough of feeling sorry for myself! I give myself one more week to get this out of my system and this fat arse is getting itself down the gym. JC, dishy doctor, is due out here in two weeks…mmmnnn not sure he's going to be looking too happy with his handy work!

18 March 2012

Ok, folks…we have a new game! The Regrowth Game! Every Saturday I'm going to post a pic so you can see how the hair's coming on. This is probably the most unattractive pic I've posted on here of myself but hey ho…Now you get to see the bald head in all its glory and watch the regrowth over the following weeks. The hospital reckons about six weeks till I get a full head of hair so…let the countdown begin.

24 March 2012

Totally overwhelmed! Thought I was off to an organic restaurant and my friends surprised me with an end-of-chemo party…not sure bursting into tears was the reaction expected! Thank you for being the absolutely most amazing friends…I am so, so lucky and there is not a day that goes by where I don't feel totally thankful.

26 March 2012

Hair update…it's not attractive but it's coming back! As is my taste for red wine strangely enough;-). Had first radiotherapy session today, it's like being zapped by a big cake mixer…well done, Marie Curie; what a legend! She discovered radiotherapy in case you didn't know…oooh it's like a lesson blog today. Don't forget to sponsor Steve Fantom and Paul Jones for their runs…Singapore half marathon and the London marathon respectively. Much love peeps.

3 April 2012

Week three of the hair-growing competition! Competition with myself that is!

4 April 2012

Radiotherapy all going well…and loving my days out with different people. I am so lucky to have such lovely people taking me…I think I may well have floundered (is that the right word?) by now without them. Am going to get some sun this weekend all be it with my right boob firmly covered…not that I'd go topless, or in fact, anyone would like to see the state of my boobs right now, might freak a few people out!

I am rocking the scarf look more and more this week. Not rocking literally as you all know me well and know that my moon face is not really designed for looking cool in a scarf. I am a cross between a biker (one that could well be related to those chefs) and an overweight cover girl, yes, I'm being light-hearted, but there is an element of truth in the look. The scarf is on more for the reason that I'm bloody scared the hair won't grow back if I don't give it a bit of breathing space. Come on fluffy hair…you can do it!

Right, off for more zapping this morning. Take care peeps and remember three green teas a day keep cancer at bay…makes you pee like an elephant but hey, needs must!

8 April 2012

If I don't write this now, I'll forget. So, three monthly check-ups with the consultant today. All good, as in, no lumps or anything and everything healing well. I thought I'd be told I've got to have a whole load more tests but no, I figure that will all be done with the oncologist now at the GICC. Well…consultant is changing hospitals, basically because of the bad care going on and would you believe it, it seems their misdiagnosing me has opened up a whole can of worms! As you know the insurance people have been difficult, to say the least saying I've had cosmetic surgery (I look like a patchwork quilt FFS) so Dr Coach (consultant and JC's mate…you all following?) is going to put a letter to the insurance company which will hopefully help. He is also best mates with the head of the company so fingers, toes, arms etc. crossed that he can work some magic. The irony of the story is Dr C. is changing hospitals to work at the…wait for it…British Cosmetic Surgery Hospital! Well, that's going to go down well when I have to see him with the insurance company, isn't it? He said he'd see me for free if there was a problem—bless! JC was out at the beginning of the week for two days and wanted to see me apparently—aw! Unfortunately, I had a migraine, missed day one of his conference, spoke at day two and then had to get a plane home.

Never mind…nipple reconstruction beckons in the summer months! Asked Dr Coach when I'd find out if the cancer had gone and he said basically I wouldn't for ten years—I'll be bloody 52…terrific! Apparently, because of the dodgy kind I have there is a big risk over the next two years, then a slightly smaller risk over the following three, and then it drops over the next five. Guess I'm going to be seeing a fair bit of hospitals! I am now on a healthy eating regime and determined to kick this thing right in the goolies! What a morning hey! Now off to Abu Dhabi for today's zapping…it's a busy day here in Dubai. Again, remember folks…three green teas a day keep cancer at bay!

8 April 2012

I think my eyelashes are growing back!

14 April 2012

Facebook not letting me update photos right now so I'm afraid you're going to have to hold tight for a growing hair update…You'll not believe it though; it's only bloody coming back grey! Jeesh! I come from a family where grey hair is not prevalent; well in all fairness Mum dyes hers (whoops…another secret out the bag) and Dad at the grand old age of 71 has only just started going grey! My grandma had hardly any grey in her 80s yet my granddad Tom had a fluffy/baldy grey look which mine is currently doing an impression of! He'd actually be pissing himself laughing at mine if he was still here! And all you buggers who told me it was going to come back thicker and lovelier are all in for it I tell you;-).

On a good note, I am now back at the gym! Nearly killed myself as pressed the effort level on the cycle by mistake-not a pretty site, but I had a spring in my step on exiting the place, nonetheless.

Off out tonight to the Armani Hotel wouldn't you know! You'll have to excuse me; false eyelashes, pencilled eyebrows and make-up beckon...now which wig to wear...

26 April 2012

No idea why but can't seem to load photos at the moment onto Facebook from my phone so there are two hair updates sitting and waiting! I think the tiredness has finally kicked in, fell asleep on Skype at the weekend (oops) and I am wondering if 8 p.m. is a little early for bed? Apart from that, all has been going well. Yet again, luck is on my side and the side effects seem to be pretty minimal. I think the tiredness is actually the toing and froing from school and getting back on top of my teaching. Anyhow...only four more treatments left finish on Tuesday! Can you Adam and Eve it! Eight months ago, my life totally changed overnight and now I'm still standing and despite the fact I have the most undesirable head of hair, I think I've worn the bruises of the past months pretty well. Love the opportunity to catch up with people each day and I could not have gotten through these six weeks without the absolute kindness and patience of my friends. I do not know what I have done to deserve such kindness from folks.

Sleeping is not great at the mo. as I seem to be suffering from the hot sweats. Could be two things: effects from the drugs or early menopause. Am gutted if it is the latter but hey—shit happens and I know I'll deal with it. I have my health right now and that has to take priority, I guess.

So…These mad months have inspired me to want to get fit and I have three things in mind if you fancy joining me: a 5k this summer, a 10k at some point in the following six months in Dubai, the moonwalk in May 2013 and wait for it…the London marathon in 2014! Now god knows if this is achievable (literally) especially as I couldn't even run for a bus right now, but I figure it's a goal and certainly beats sitting on my backside doing nothing. It also allows me to get myself fit for two reasons…to beat this baby with a stick and to be the fittest I have ever been in my life—it can only help keep cancer at bay! If you fancy joining me in any of these tasks…yay! And if you think I've gone mental—well, you might well be right.

Fi and Karen arrive tomorrow and am dead excited to have them over…A little bit of home to keep me going till July. Much love people and hopefully the photos will appear soon, when the phone decides the time is right! Oh, I forgot to say…Paul Jones and Steve and Archie Fantom…You are my absolute heroes and inspiration!

29 April 2012

I have one thing to say today…it's too bloody hot to wear a wig! Who'd get cancer in Dubai, hey? Rubbish!

2 May 2012

Well…the last one was meant to be my last post for a while, but my goodness I had to share my lovely morning with you. Arrived at the staff briefing this morning to everyone cheering and the common room filled with pink balloons and cupcakes…two surprises in as many months! Thank you, lovely people…

Btw…Seem to be able to upload photos again so the hair race has been updated for you all. The most recent one was today…not attractive in any form, but it is coming back…slowly and grey, but hey, it's hair!

2 May 2012

Three operations, six cycles of chemotherapy, six weeks of radiotherapy…In the words of some good friends…Boom! Eight months ago I went to a hospital to insist I had a delayed mammogram because I'd found a lump back in March 2011…today I walked out of my last radiotherapy session! I cannot believe what has happened to me; slightly too much to comprehend at the moment but needless to say, that's all, folks! Four months of rest and looking after myself properly and then the scans! Oh! Four months of rest…you are most welcome. Thank you peeps for dragging me through these last eight months; your kindness, support, humour, hugs, slaps…Your name, it will never be forgotten.

Now's the part where I go quiet for a while, print this blog off and take in what's happened to me!

Huge, huge hugs and more love than I could muster to you all. You very special people who have read and supported me with your comments deserve a medal.

9 May 2012

Off to fight another battle today…this time with the hospital regarding the misdiagnosis that could have killed me! God this is one journey I'm telling you! I think they think I'm a bit of a pushover as well…don't mess with the Hitch is what I say to this one!

2 June 2012

Right people…May 2013…who's going to do the moonwalk with me? I've registered my interest and suggest you guys do the same but would love to get a team of us together. The final dates will be announced in September and by that time we need a team name and an agreement on our rough finishing time so that we can walk together. I know it's a big, big ask, but would absolutely love to do this with a team of us.

So…let's get planning :-)!

3 June 2012

Slowly but surely, it's coming back…not the best photo need photo but keeps you all up to date :-). It's well into the 40s over here and the wigs are getting a bit uncomfortable, not quite confident to go without yet, but I'll get there. Health-wise feeling good—running and swimming and loving it.

Hopefully, back to the hospital this week for more fighting, have been in contact and met with a couple of solicitors who all seem to think I have a good case. If I can get rid of the insurance debt that still hangs over me life will be much grander!

Cannot wait to get back to the UK to see you all, although rest assured, I have been well and truly looked after by my Dubai family. I just wish I could have you all in the same country—that would be one fab party!

Lots of love to you all and sorry UK people for taking so long to update…big hugs.

29 June 2012

Ok, people…first of the fundraising! Walk Ten is a 10k walk on Saturday 11 August, starting at 7 p.m. followed by a firework display at 10 p.m. at Denbies Wine Estate, Dorking. It'll be a good starting point for the moonwalk Team Hitch and it's £10 to register…all the money goes towards funding Marie Curie nurses. I am more than happy to register and pay on my card for any of you who are up for this…I know it's holiday time so it could just be you and me Mum! And maybe Anne Petrie :-)? Maybe we can convince Dad and David Petrie to fire up the BBQ and have a few drinks back at Robin Hood Road afterwards! If you're interested, let me know and I'll do the registering. A great positive step towards a year of Team Hitch fundraising for the Big C! P.S. eyelashes back :-), eyebrows coming back, hair on head coming back slowly…other hair growing far too quickly for my liking! Big love!

2 July 2012

Off to Chessington today, very excited to be seeing special friends and have a good giggle…thought I'd share a lovely quote from Mum with you! The conversation goes like this, "Have a good time…got your wig on?"

"No, Mum. Got a scarf on. Was worried it might fall off on the rides."

"Hahahahahahaha, I'd love to see that! Hahahahaha."

Only in the Hitchcock family!

9 July 2012

Ultrasound was clear! I am a paranoid bloody wreck after all! Thank god! Now can look forward to getting my nipple on Thursday :-)

10 July 2012

Absolutely loving being home and getting lots of fresh air, especially after all that Dubai heat…mind you, saying that, got absolutely soaked yesterday while out with Wendy. We literally looked like someone had poured a bucket of water on each of us! Am off to the hospital today for an ultrasound on my tummy, which has been a little sore for quite a while now. Ordinarily, this would never have bothered me but today I'm nervous, to say the least. I've become a paranoid wreck and every twinge, ache; twitch has my head wondering if it's a little cell growing in a new place! This one is particularly worrying as it happens to be right where my pancreas is…so should not have done Internet research—what a doughnut! Will keep you posted. I'm back at the McIndoe on Thursday for 'finishing up'…On the upside of that one, I have the dishy doc JC to look forward to seeing! Hair's steadily coming back and I've done the scarf thing far more often than the wig over here…Am willing a few more inches so I can get away with nothing although look like a boy which is not thrilling in any shape or form. Am trying desperately to embrace this new look…mmmmn, cute pixie crop it ain't!

12 July 2012

A double-edged sword day today…back to the McIndoe to see lovely JC for a new nipple! This will involve a tweak of the skin to provide the nipple (not quite sure how that's going to work) and the tattoo of the areola…You'd think I could have chosen something a little more stylish than that and a pair of eyebrows for my first tattoos hey?

Have discovered another bloody lump on the reconstructed breast as well…hoping this is scar tissue as it is right in the corner at the inside bit of the wire (girlies will understand) but will get JC to have a look. There are some days when I think it's all in my head and I so don't want to make a fuss, but this is a definite lump of sorts. There could be further reconstruction done but apparently that's going to be done next week…If you ask me, I think JC is pretty excited about me being home and would just like to see me every week;-).

No general[7] today, just a local and an in/out procedure. What poor JC doesn't realise though is that when I'm nervous I can talk the hind legs off a donkey, he's only had to work on me when I've been out up until now…good luck I say!

Well folks…hopefully at the end of today, I will look a little more like a woman again and I can't wait :-).

12 July 2012

Me again…No new nipple for Sally today I'm afraid. JC has decided there is a bit of neatening up to do and will do everything at once, either next Wed or Sat. JC…stop making excuses to see me! Hilarious moment of the day sat for at least five minutes with my boobs out while having a normal conversation with JC! Desperately wanted to cover up but didn't want to look like a prude!!! Can you imagine talking about insurance etc. with your tits out? How life has changed.

---

[7] Anaesthetic

JC has decided to take some more away from the reconstructed boob which I'm glad of, it is way bigger than the other and he also wants to neaten up the reduced boob—all under local! Wonder how many times I'll have to go to the loo before I leave next week! Sorry boys for the boob honesty, but remember sharing is caring;-).

18 July 2012

Preparing for the fifth operation of the year…a local in the operating theatre…could be interesting. Do you think they know I always need the loo when I'm nervous? Let's get tomorrow over and done with, please!

Last sharing is caring…So, Mum and Dad revealed to me that the ride home might be a bit squashed as they purchased a parasol for the garden while I was having my op! 'You'll be alright, just squash up a bit, it was a good bargain!' Hahahahaha! Loving the folks, what with that and the involuntary farts they've provided, they have kept me very entertained!

21 July 2012

No local after all. Full-on general! Veins playing up but managed to get one on the fifth attempt. I have a nipple! Yay!

1 August 2012

Well, the new nip is doing well…if you ask me, it looks like someone stubbed a fag out on my boob, but apparently, it will shrink to the right size! In the grand scheme of things, I'm starting to look pretty normal. JC is a miracle worker! Just the tattoo on the 16 August and then we're done. The lovely Amanda took me today. I think Amanda secretly wanted to ogle JC and that she did! Can't wait for the first Team Hitch walk on the 11 August and can't thank you all enough for the fab sponsorship.

9 August 2012

And don't forget…first fundraiser for cancer is this Saturday for Team Hitch, if you want to sponsor us please do—the link's on my home page and huge thanks to those of you that already have. This year of fundraising means even more to me, four very dear friends have lost their lovely mums to this bloody horrid disease and another their dad and my lovely daddy is right in the middle of all of his tests! One of my friends told me, 'Cancer doesn't choose you!' I am absolutely committed to this cause and to raise as much money over the next 12 months as we can…Go, Team Hitch!

13 August 2012

I love my new nipple! Just thought I'd put that out there!

16 August 2012

Well…I got myself a new tattoo today—bet you can't guess what it is;). Needless to say, all things considered, I love my new boobie—it now looks like the other one! How clever those people are at the McIndoe Surgical Centre in East Grinstead. I am totally indebted to the care and patience the lovely JC has shown me and today learnt a little more about this amazing, amazing man.

JC has four children; two of them have cystic fibrosis! JC's eldest daughter May is awaiting a double lung transplant but due to the lack of people on the organ donor list this is proving difficult—she has been on the list for over a year. Can you imagine? This amazing man has not only saved my life but he has made what could have been a horrible, horrible experience more than bearable. At times, quite frankly, he's made it interesting and funny! He does this for loads of people all the time yet can't help his own daughter. It seems dreadfully unfair. Please, please, please if you haven't already, consider going on the organ donor list. I'm going to post a link on my main page, it was something I did when I was first diagnosed and was unsure what was in store for me. Thanks for listening and if one person registers (you can do it online) my little plea has gone a long way. Lots of love peeps! We need to be careful here. Should we ask JC's permission to include it? It's very personal information…

22 August 2012

Team Hitch raised over £1,500 for Marie Curie.

25 August 2012

Today is all about Team Hitch! My darling dad has been diagnosed with prostate cancer! What a bloody year it's been! He has a little in his lymph nodes and a little in his bones, but they think it is treatable and more importantly controllable. We are of a very similar vein my dad and I, and as usual, there is laughter and giggles in the Hitchcock House. And I know, above all, that he will conquer this and remain absolutely positive.

The interesting thing is that the nurse said to my folks today that they are researching into links between prostate and breast cancer. This would explain a lot as it still remains an absolute mystery as to why I have BC. My dad's dad had prostate cancer so it could well be that the genes come from that line rather than my mum's, seems I take after my dad in more ways than one. The only difference is that dad's is hormone related and mine is most definitely not. At least, I have been home for this and not worrying in Dubai, good timing, Dad!

Please spare a thought for my poor mum in all of this. As most of you know, my dad and I have a reputation for winding my mum up and thinking we're highly hilarious!! Poor thing, having a daughter going through cancer treatment is bad enough without having your husband diagnosed as well. It makes this year of fundraising even more precious to me. Over £1500 raised by 'Team Hitch' for Marie Curie, two events for Macmillan in Dubai to organise and then the big moonwalk in May. All systems go and back to the gym for me, I have a 10k run to do and a marathon to walk…oh and the channel to swim (at least I'm out of the bloody harbour now)!

31 August 2012

Today, it would seem, is a good day! School have now done a fabulous thing and gone with Bupa insurance! I was able to have a normal conversation with a lovely lady in the UK who could understand me, and I could understand her. Not at any point did she make me feel that I was a second-class citizen and she was sympathetic to my worries, efficient at sorting the approval for my oncologist appointment and willing to go above the call of duty. After the crap that has happened this last year, this is just fabulous!

Another good thing—I got Dr Coach to look at the little lump on my reconstructed breast that's been bothering me a little. JC told me it was nothing to worry about and right he was. It was my bloody rib I could feel! I kid you not—what a doughnut! God, never been able to feel those before! The joys of small boobies people!

And last bit of good news today my desk has arrived, which will eventually go in my spare room when I've tidied :-). I am preparing to pen my blog after much encouragement from family, friends, doctors and nurses.

I still have a way to go on my journey and will continue to keep this going but I'm ready to now commit some of this to paper in the hope that one day it just may help someone to see the lighter side.

It is so lovely to be feeling like Shitcock again—my, I've missed her! Feeling the love today.

31 August 2012

Bloods done—yay! Now for an appointment with the consultant, JC's friend then Abu Dhabi on Sunday…mmmmnn sounding familiar! How I loved my summer of near normality! Fingers crossed, guys…Just the scans to get through over the next couple of weeks and the results to wait for. I am hoping, praying and wishing for some good news!

3rd September 2012

I have some good news for you all. I went to Abu Dhabi today, my blood is 'perfect' I seem to be in great health, and I've been given the 'see you for a follow-up in three months!' I am so, so happy. No need for a PET scan until next April apparently and my oncologist is really pleased with me! I'll post more when I've had time to digest it, but have been in tears today with the good news and the fact I can now start to get back to normal! Wow, wow, wow and thank you, thank you, thank you to all of you for getting me through the last year! Lots and lots of love xxxxxx

P.S. should have known this little chap would have bought me good luck! Photo? Perhaps footnote.

7 September 2012

A year ago today, I was told it was more than likely I had breast cancer, would most definitely have to have chemotherapy and make sure I took someone with me for the results! I was sobbing! What a bloody year hey and can't believe I am out the other end! Yay!

28 October 2012

Dear all...The date for the moonwalk has just been announced as 11 May 2013. Registration hasn't been opened yet, but Team Hitch gets the date in your diaries and boys, let's get your bras :-). We're going to do this! £2553 raised so far, just think what we can do :-).

Life is good at the mo. Health-wise, just a routine mammogram and tests in December, but apart from the niggle tummy feeling, I'm back to my old self. The hair is a problem; however, lovely people are this is not a haircut that works in Dubai. I have, however, discovered the straightness (not sure what she means here—hair?) again and I promise you I am trying to embrace it, but still feel like a twat anytime I wear a dress! My jeans, coat and Converse would suit the look so much better, but the chances of that out here are slim, to say the least.

I find it hard to believe what I was going through a year ago and I don't mind admitting that over the last few weeks,

I've found everything I've been through a little overwhelming. The charity stuff is good though, gives me a focus and makes me feel like I'm giving a little back. I have a feeling the 12th is going to be a hard day, a year to the day I spent nine hours in an operating theatre! I look forward to getting through this year and being able to reflect properly at some point. A few tears today when I was called a boy (probably quite innocently) have made me realise that perhaps things are rooted a little deeper than I thought. I'll get there I promise. I am one of the lucky ones!

My wonderful dad is doing well. His levels have dropped from 88 to 11 (SP levels…mmmmnnn, not sure what that means) and that is fab. He is having his injections and will continue to do so, but hearing Mum and Dad arguing on the phone yesterday makes me think things are back to normal in the Hitchcock household!

Take care, keep an eye out for the registration dates for the Moonwalk and drink green tea!

15 November 2012

It would seem that the online application for the moonwalk is now full so it's posted all the way. If you're nervous about doing the full marathon (I'm shitting it—sorry Mum!), my mum has signed up for the Half-Moon and would like the company. She has signed for the maximum time which means we can all start together. If you do want to join Team Hitch for the full moon or the half-moon, you can still do a postal application for the full or online for the half. Places do fill quickly though so hurry, hurry and let us make a difference to this bloody awful disease! Big love and hugs to you all.

7 December 2012

First of the routine check-ups today, mammogram and ultrasound. Fifteen months ago this was the scan where the doctor and radiographer first prepared me for the year to come. Same radiographer and doctor today, but apart from a few lumps and bumps that need keeping an eye on I'm all clear! Tears again today but these ones for a very different reason. Absolutely chuffed to bits! I don't mind telling you I have been shitting myself about today. Bloods next week and further results from those on the 17, so fingers, toes, arms, legs and anything else you fancy crossing for those and a lovely Christmas, and I even have hair this year :-). What a bloody lovely day!

18 December 2012

Second all-clear today! Blood perfect...borderline on the Vitamin D and Calcium so on pills and attempting to sort diet accordingly but all good! Chuffed to absolute bits. It's beginning to feel a lot like Christmas! Now for Daddy Hitchcock's results tomorrow this would mean a wonderful celebration back in the UK! Off ice skating to celebrate...Oh yes, I am!

18 December 2012

Good news...Dad's blood has gone down to single figures! Happy Christmas everyone! I am soooooooo looking forward to a great big hug with my mum and dad and a Christmas with hair and smiles...and this year I'll be able to taste the dinner! Cannot wait!

1 January 2013

Just want to say a big thank you to u all for getting me through 2012…Some of you have to literally drag me through it at times. I don't want to dwell, but your funny comments and ongoing love have been more than anyone could ask for and I could not have done it without you. Thank you, 'special' Facebook people I am raising a glass to you all, looking forward to 2013 and everything it has to offer! Love you lots and a very Happy New Year! Xxxxxxx

25 April 2013

Got the all-clear! Now onto six monthly check-ups! Dr Rates had a good feel of the boobs and all the blood had come back 'perfect!' I am over the moon…now onto the moonwalk;-). Happy St George's Day. I certainly feel like I've slain the dragon!

4 June 2013

Ultrasound six monthly today…All Clear! Very Happy, Hitchcock!

10 June 2013

Sad day today saying goodbye to Dr. Coach, my breast consultant over here and the guy who diagnosed me. Have always thought he was a little bit autistic (not sure I should say that) but after the great big hug he gave me today, maybe I was wrong!—Legalities. Should we change the name?

One little op next week to have my Portacath removed and that's me done in the UAE. Lots of mixed feelings especially as I'm going to have to start again with docs who don't know me and haven't seen me throughout my treatment…although as my ultrasound doctor said, I'm going home to some of the best docs in the world!

Be sure I'll put some pics of this next op on next week and then I think the title of this page should read, 'Sally Got Better' and I need to get off Facebook and get writing!

Happy Sunday, people!

18 June 2013

And this is what they took out of me today![8] Only a local and I heard every bit of it…Yuk! Not so good when you see the clip things to hold you open pass in front of you! Thought I was going to vomit! On top of that, they had me wired up so I could hear my heartbeat! Now this was quite funny, and I did have a bit of personal entertainment on the operating table trying to make it go faster and slower…am wondering if that's a bit wrong. The doctor was lovely and chatted throughout! He even knew James Burton…Imagine having that conversation on an operating table! Anyhow—the magic button is gone. The last op fingers crossed! Happy days and thank you Evelyn Matafonov for looking after me! Btw, I took the Portacath as a souvenir! Hahaha!

31 August 2013

The journey begins today. Sitting in a hospital in the UK waiting to see my new breast consultant. Lady next to me eating a packet of chocolate raisins really, really loudly! With a horn as her text sounds! The hospital is nice…not quite as opulent as the one in Dubai and you'll be pleased to know I have sorted at long last my Bupa cover out—costing an arm

---

[8] Photo not available

and a leg mind. But at least I know should anything happen again I can go to the McIndoe without it costing me a mortgage. Missing my Dubai buddies today! Oh my god…lady next to me now drinking really loudly too. She's just got the look and put the raisins down—quietly now Mrs, else I'll be having a word! Oh no, the raisins are up again!

Fingers crossed for a good result today and a nice new consultant. And even bigger fingers crossed for my dad who is really poorly in hospital. Bloody cancer…nasty thing. Please leave my family alone now!

Part 3

31 August 2013

…Bloody cancer…nasty thing, please leave my family alone now!

20 July 2014

Please excuse my self-indulgence in posting daily again here, but my blog provided a great avenue for me and allowed me to keep you all up to date with the funny stories of Hitch treatment!

So, it would seem that he up there feels I'm strong enough to enter another little fight and fight I will folks. This week has been a little bit of a shell shock and you guessed it…those little cancer cells have been doing their business in my body again! Buggers! A little over a month ago I started to lose feeling in my left hand…This progressed rapidly and after eventually being referred to A and E on Tuesday a brain scan took place and sure enough the little buggers had out themselves all the way up there—they must have well pushed themselves in—it's a big brain! A whole-body scan has revealed they have been working hard and nestled themselves in all kinds of little places. So…What next? Well…the brain is the priority…mainly due to the lack of hand movement, which is debilitating, to say the least. Radiotherapy will start on this in the next couple of weeks. After that, possible oral chemo, but as the oncologist says, one thing at a time! And an assessment after each treatment. The hair will come out from the radiotherapy this time but not the chemo—you kind of have to see the funny side with that one! So, yesterday, I had the drastic chop from my wonderful hairdresser and buddy John! I kind of love it and will post a pic for you! Thought I'd get the shock factor in early this time round and the wigs will be restyled next week. Don't you worry…I intend to do this in style again and I will be wearing my Manolo Blahniks throughout! The biggest bummer to all of this is my driver's licence is now void for two years! Does anyone need a Black Ford KA? My poor mum is currently in possession of three cars and is the only person able to drive in the Hitch household! Takes 'Driving Miss Daisy' to a whole new level! Please don't feel you have to stay attached to this group…Self-indulgence can be pretty boring, but I know some of you want a regular update and the phone can be a little overwhelming some days. Juicing, online shopping and celebrating each and every day…here I come!

21 July 2014

Day 2 of The Hitch Challenge and thank god for the fan in my bedroom which has allowed six hours of sleep! Yay! Yesterday was a busy old day and possibly the first I've felt a little frustrated. Menial tasks like putting on my knickers, bra and earrings are a nightmare! I was talking to Jo T last night and it's true, if this was just a broken arm or a trapped nerve I'd deal with it, but the fact it's linked to the brain makes it seem much worse than it is—I need to overcome this a little and I am going to do some Pilates breathing stretches with my arms and shoulders to help myself! That'll be a nice sight in a few minutes! My poor dad was not so good yesterday which of course another blow is in our little family life. I tried to tell him my predicament—I don't know if that was selfish or not, but I wanted to fire the fight in him. When mum asked him to repeat what I'd told him, he replied, "There's been some problems in Wales with blood tests!" You have to giggle…we did.

When I eventually explained, the little buggers were back and we were both sitting there with matching probs he replied, "That's a bit shit." Family room in the hospice anyone! I know it's crass but Dad and I will always see the funny side to this, it's our coping mechanism. We also reminded Mum that she wasn't allowed to join our club! At least that made Dad giggle which was a sight I needed to see. So, today should be radiotherapy mapping at the hospital for me for my brain radiotherapy which should start on the 28 July. Am still waiting for insurance approval…obviously—fuckers! (Sorry Mum) but at least if it doesn't go through, I'll be referred to the NHS ASAP…slightly less Russian roulette than the Dubai debacle. Another plus yesterday was my first-ever online shop! Now without a car and the ability to lift with both hands, I feel this is the way forward. Delivered right to the front door and was brilliant! Should have done these years ago!! Now to get mum on to it as well…Neil waited in with me just in case there were any problems with carrying etc. but the lovely Sainsbury's man carried it with no probs! Lots of healthy organic fodder to boost my body up! And an array of vitamins from the organic health shop to boot too! I told you all, I'll do all I can to help this. Right, I'm off to shower…could be a while and then the knickers, bra, and make-up scenario starts again! It's ok…I slept with the earrings in—one job done!

Helen is taking me today so a good meeting about 'A Taste of the Business' too to take my mind off all this shit. Have a good day peeps…eat well, exercise sensibly and visit your doctor! Just saying…xxx

22 July 2014

Yesterday was a challenging one. The mapping for the brain radiotherapy and mask-making were absolutely fine, actually…better than expected! The realisation of this crazy, stupid diagnosis then took its toll and try as I did not to, I got myself completely stressed. In true Hitch style, I had a shower and thought a bit of make-up etc. might help the normality, but then, flashing lights, a totally numb arm and my face started to drop = panic! It was similar to the experience I had after Pilates when this all started! I breathed, relaxed and eventually got myself back to some kind of normality. It was a wake-up call though and made me realise that I need to be careful. I have a list of numbers by the front door and will call the ambulance if it happens again. I also intend to do a bit of meditation, deep breathing and stretching each morning in the hope of taming the brain monkeys! Little critters! Anyhow, off down to Woking this morning to sort some bits and see my dear buddy Jo T who's flown down from Manchester (said with accent) and later on Jo G (said again with accent;)). A visit with Dad in the hope he is feeling better—so up and down and heartbreaking to see. We seem to be overwhelmed as a family right now so I'm going on my positive mantra to conjure up some good things. A little ditty to keep you smiling…Steroids have blocked me up—inappropriate farting ahoy! Some things never change!

22 July 2014

Possibly up there on the hard scale factor! Met Jo T at Woking station, her bus and my train arrived in perfect time and my brave wonderful mum came and picked us up. Got bits sorted with Mum at home and then had a meeting with one of the most amazing men I will probably ever meet in my life! His name is Manolo and he works with the doctors and hospice and is our[9] palliative care person. He is fab! There is no doubt my humour was a shock at first for him—poor love! But his helpfulness, advice and support of a family in utter crisis make him a man who should be wearing medals! I certainly wouldn't want to be doing his job…talking about death on a daily basis with people and the choices to make while the mind is sane.

Thank god, Jo was with us to write everything down and to help us take in all the shit we need to understand. There were real tears today…which was probably a little relief to Manolo. But! There were very funny moments too. The suggestion of a suppository for my blocked stomach did the trick quickly…inappropriate farting was gone (well not strictly true) and the mini moment I suffered last night was probably due to cutting down the steroids by half—not slowly but too quickly! Poor body. Actually feel loads better now! As I say…the meeting was hard but positive and I have a much clearer view of the road in front. I will need support over the coming weeks and need to accept my independence may be compromised a little but so many people have offered to help and I will spend a little more time at Mum's…to annoy her of course! Dad was a little more upbeat today but hates

_____

[9] 'Our' is referring to Sally and her dad, John.

one of the nurses ('miserable old cow' he calls her to which we 'shush' him up). In all fairness, she does look a bit sour-faced!

This evening was positively perfect though and I feel guilty for saying as much. Jo G and Danny made a four-hour round trip down to Surbs for supper and cups of tea and for a few hours it felt like there was nothing wrong. Grateful is not a big enough word! Thanks to each and every one of you for your support at the moment. I'm trying so hard to call/text and fail miserably, but I do listen to my messages and thank you all from the bottom of my heart! And the folks too! Jo T is on night watch…Medical notes are now in a folder…just in case! And I'm feeling a little more settled. Good night all and appreciate every minute always!

23 July 2014

And another little blow to us all. We are still smiling, laughing and having Jo T as Hitchcock's PA has been more than a blessing for the three of us these past two days! Poor girl is going to need counselling when she gets back up north! Tonight's scratch card purchases were without a doubt high comedy! That, my friends, is humour at its highest and best—a severe loss to the wallet! So, from this, I'm thinking of new show ideas for my media mogul friends…you know who you are! 'The Hospice?' I'm quite serious…fuck 'One Born Every Minute' (sorry for swearing, Mum). This is genius! Xxx we need to discuss! Thank you, as always for your energy, love and support at these difficult times.

25 July 2014

Tired, emotional, working a little too late and in need of a rest. Bar another little kick in the shins from a simply sparkling email and a Dad so desperate to see his garden one last time, there will still be giggles to be had between the tears! I suppose there are days you just put everything in life into perspective. I will be back on form tomorrow—that is a promise! And thank you, those of you who have tirelessly ferried me around today, listening to my moans and my incessant swearing of the really bad word! Sorry, Mum! It is more appreciated than you know! Love you. And Mum…you are an inspiration to the world, even if your parking is a bit panicky.

Well, I did it…I've been! Had the most wonderful reflexology and faced my demons at the same time! Even had a giggle and met some amazing people! I even have a mahoosive fundraising idea and I think I'm on it with this one. Leave it with me folks. Dad is so incredibly poorly right now and spending time with him is the most important thing in my day. I told him today I needed him to be brave, to try out all this shit and be strong so I can draw on his strength. He still makes me giggle mind and his phrase of the day was 'I'm just bloody browned-off mate…that's what I am!' I'm not surprised, my darling dad, I'm not bloody surprised!

This evening was productive beyond belief and I just feel blessed with everyone's support and help at the mo. Talking honestly and openly about such dreadful things is just shit beyond belief, but we figured tonight there was a reason. I have a plan…one I won't share right now—but there has to be a reason and I think I might have the grand plan figured out in some obscure way! Thanks, Jo and Mark for helping me figure that out tonight!

I go to bed tonight wishing two beautiful people a lovely wedding tonight and wishing I was up in the lakes with you all celebrating! Have the most fantastic, fantastic day and sending you all the love and happiness in the world! Night all.

P.S. The lady at the hospice today asked me where I get all my strength and positivity from…easy, I said…"I like to giggle!" Go giggle, people! And make happy memories!

26 July 2014

Emotionally drained today on every level but a giggle to share with you…In order to cheer my darling daddy up today, Wendy and I became the 'Chuckle Nurses'. This is the biggest smile I've seen from my hero in weeks!

28 July 2014

So, we arrive at the hospital to find Dad fast asleep, legs a kimbo and hanging out of his hospital bed (please pray, think positively or draw on anything you can for a smooth transition to the hospice tomorrow for my darling daddy). In Hitch style and without much patience right now I went straight to the nurses and asked them to help sort Dad and at least make him comfortable. Eventually, we got Dad comfortable and sorted and Mum went about giving him a freshen-up and a shave…All the time my dad looking forlorn and sad, not really with it. As soon as we were on our own, he opened one eye and said, "Have they gone?" Mum and I reply, "Yes!" To which he raises his fist and says, "Yes…did it!"

It is at this point that Dad confesses…he has been so fed up and the socks and the airbags on his legs have been driving him crazy that he spent the hour prior to our arrival enacting a Houdini escape plan…hence the state we found him in! We were wetting ourselves! Nice one, Dad! Mum spent the whole day at the hospital with him today and I think it's probably what they both need. It's not a great ward, and although everyone's nice enough, there's just not the care that Dad needs…That and the fact he is still 'browned off!' I can't even begin to imagine how he feels facing his own death and it scares me shitless that I have this to come! Bloody cancer! I nearly said the F word Mum but held it in! Telling someone who is like family today, who looked after me in Dubai was heartbreaking…and I think it's the first time I've sobbed big fat tears as I've done the reaper speech! Not for me, but for my dad and my mum as well.

There are just times right now when I kind of hate the world and wonder what the Hitch's did to be living in this hell—answers on a postcard! I'm sure there are some suggestions! Tomorrow is a big day: the start of the radiotherapy, the start of a new business and two weeks where I have to be around people and not on my own—you can probably imagine my independent annoyed face right now!

Green tea, cereal and Gogi berries with an antioxidant juice ready for brekkie…let's do this folks! I'll bloody show those sneaky little cells who's boss!

29 July 2014

Dad happy. Tired, but happy! Toenails…not even going down that story line-gag, gag, gag!

ATOTB—Going well this week…tired, but still at it! One-fifth of the radiotherapy on the brain complete! Today as I lay underneath the scanner with my head screwed to the board, I wondered how my brain was coping. Bar the blurry vision, which is still apparent, I reckon it's all good—that and the fact the hand is still refusing to work its magic!

A lovely supper with Alan Bradshaw and then whisked off to be looked after at Broughton Towers Prefab again! Feeling very looked after right now on so many levels and coping surprisingly well with the lack of independence—not quite sure that's going to last! Thank you, everyone xx

30 July 2014

Big fat period—welcome! With one hand! You're having a bloody laugh, aren't you? Jeesh! If you can't find me this week people, I'm in the bog performing magic! New show idea for Edinburgh perhaps? Xx

31 July 2014

Inspired and knackered! I think musicals might be quite hard to watch…had a right little tear at Wicked this evening! Followed by a lovely chinwag with my gorgeous buddy Katie Rowley Jones.

2 August 2014

And yesterday was pretty amazing. The ATOTB course finished with a bang and somehow…with a lot of goodwill, patience and friendship we got through it. People have been amazing this week and I can't thank you all enough. Dad promised me he'd stay strong this week and he has…just goes to show what you can do. Now as for the face—well that's another story! It is fat! It is moonlike! And quite frankly that and my arm are pissing me off beyond belief! The face got so fat that the mask I wear for radiotherapy is now tight! Well, tighter than it was! Bummer! My chin seems to link my face and neck now too! Not pretty! I'm rather hoping this will pass as the steroids are nearly out now. Have gone from 8 a day to 1 a day. Don't panic, I've followed the doctor's orders, but because the steroids were making no difference to my hand it was ok to cut them.

Generally, I feel ok and the blurry vision, touch wood, has not been awful either, possibly a little better. Maybe those critters are shrinking nicely. I just need my hand back. I feel so blessed for never having had a disability in my life…I really need to learn from others on this one about a) getting on with it and b) getting over the moaning! Kerry Coburn recalled the Kill Bill opening to me the other day so every day I am trying to create brain magic on the hand I imagine myself doing an Uma! I will do this! The hand is the only difference from when the cancer first came. I never really had anything to show before bar smaller boobs and a flatter stomach—physically I was ok. The hand is a constant reminder of what is happening to me and I think that's the thing that pisses me off the most!

Anyhow…off to see Dad this morning, catch up with one of my besties this afternoon and more rest at the folks. Mum and I finished our evening last night with a little plate of cheese and biscuits (yes, I know that won't help the fat face) and a glass of organic red with a toast to Dad! He'll hate the fact he missed that cheese and biscuits!

3 August 2014

Precious time with Dad and Mum and time in my hometown eating Arabic lunch, coffee and cake with some of my favourite people! Food is still up there—*awkward fat face* followed by a good night's sleep at the folks. Today is steroid-free—let's do this! And perhaps a chance for moon faces to subside a little. Dad talked some proper weird shit today, about a Jack Russell he has bought to look after us that's coming in two weeks! It's like watching your dad on drugs! His humour is still brilliant! But I watch and wonder how many of these traits I will show when the time comes. I am without a doubt my dad's daughter so from that point of view…Look forward to the weird shit—could be good fun!

4 August 2014

I think I can honestly say I have never felt this tired in my life! It's like being in a constant state of jet lag. On top of this, I seem to have developed narcolepsy and am falling asleep everywhere…including the hospice—what must they think of me? Dad's stories keep getting better and a phone call from him regaling his morning fart had me rolling on the floor. In fact, to hear him laugh like that was just wonderful! The nurses are so lovely there and they love Dad! He's an easy man to love, my dad! He has sussed out that a few people have passed away while he's been in there. With a quick calculation of beds and deaths with Mum yesterday, he announces, "Jeesh, the odds here are not too good are they!" It's moments like this, that it becomes clear what a great big, massive, silent elephant in the room my dad is facing! To say it scares me is perhaps an understatement!

Back to radiotherapy for me today! Let's hope that bloody mask fits on the fat face and let's get these little critters shrinking away and giving me back my hand! Oh, to do a button and tie a lace again! Enjoy your hands and fingers today folks and a little jazz hand for good measure!

6 August 2014

Sorry for the delay but it would seem the radiotherapy has affected me a little after all! I slept 16 hours after Monday's session! Even folding a top required a laydown—you've not seen anything so pathetic in your life! On top of that, the radiographer said my head's a bit sore…You know it never felt it till he said, so last night I went to bed covered in Aqueous cream—I tell you, I'm up there on the attractive stakes and if one more person swishes their long blonde hair in front of me I might pull it, so watch out! My gorgeous godson came to radiotherapy with me on Monday. The staff were just magical with him. He watched the whole thing, saw my brain, tried on my superhero mask and even spoke to me halfway through treatment to tell me he loved me over the speaker…precious moments indeed and honest conversations about cancer. Including the best quote ever, 'I don't want to go to Dubai—you get cancer there'.

I wonder, young Max, I wonder! You certainly put up with a lot of stress and shit there, that's for sure. On top of this, each day with Dad is very precious. There have been a lot of honest chats with us all and the doctors and there is no doubt Dad is an extremely poorly man. Tears, laughter and general emotions are abundant. He is worried about me and mum, we are worried about him, and mum is worried about us both! It seems sad for one little family to have so much happening all at once. This was made clearer Monday when I saw my lovely breast consultant who said very honestly, "You need a miracle, Sally."

"No shit, Sherlock." One last little thing, please don't be angry if I haven't returned your calls, I have every intention, every day, but if I don't answer, I'm with Dad, having my brain zapped or asleep. I promise I will get back to you and I do think about you all and appreciate all the love and thoughts. Despite everything, I know I am very lucky and surrounded by love! Now, enough of the soppy shit go have a good day!

7 August 2014

Right, you lot! You can all pack in the crying and soppy shit else you're going to start me off on a journey of it. Let's get one thing straight—I want my life filled with laughter and many more funny stories. I have spoken to the radiographers at Guildford about finding some like-minded people. It would seem that I am part of a non-existent group and this is what I want to stRt looking at. Quite rightly there is a lot of support for children. Thanks to many charities I'm privileged to know 'Emma's Bubble Trust' and the 'Tommy D Project' that provide some seriously needed support for teenagers and young adults. There seems to be this grey area though for my kind of age. I suppose a lot of people my age have husbands and children who they immerse themselves in at times like this. But there have to be some like-minded people out there, people who fancy getting together and can actually see the funny side to this crock of shit. I'm determined to look into this and try and put some effort into finding these people. The lady at the hospice told me at any time there is probably only one out of ten of our age group[10]. Quite good statistics compared to Dad's calculations on his odds.

There's a new hospice opening in 2016 and it would be nice to put something in place there for the 'funny' group. And media moguls—I'm still convinced you are missing a

---

[10] Sally was 44 at the time

trick with a programme called 'The Hospice' it is a funny place—if you've seen what mum and I have seen these last two weeks—this is organic comedy at its absolute best! I know that sounds wrong but dying does not have to be filled with tears and sadness…surely it is a celebration of all things that are good and funny. Maybe I talk out of turn and I'm just very lucky to be part of the comedy trio that is Mum, Dad and I. There is no denying that our sense of humour can be slightly odd and inappropriate at times!

Having just done a quick re-read, there are a couple of spelling errors I've left in! They read like little farts on the page so I've left them for you. Thanks for all the love and cuddles…Yesterday was a particularly cuddly day and I got to meet Anna's little Aya for cuddles. She is adorable and as nosey and windy as her mummy—perfect!

8 August 2014

I don't know what it is about 5 a.m.! Ridiculous time to wake up. Today I have a little treat for you all…the wonderful radiographers in Guildford (I adore this team of people) let Jo T loose with the camera, so you can see what my life has been like for the last two weeks. Please excuse the double-chinned fat face, but the lasers do make me look like a superhero! Now need to come up with a superhero name: Fatty Face? Moon Girl? Farty Pants…the list is endless.

Well enjoy the pics; the last one today not quite sure the mask will last much longer with my growing cheeks and chin! And let's throw all our positive thoughts at those brain mets being reduced by a good amount.

Little story for you; the taxi man yesterday asked me what was wrong with me. I wasn't dribbling btw, he was just a bit fascinated by the hospice-to-hospital journey—had just been with Dad. When I told him my diagnosis, he was of course 'sorry' and then asked if I was hoping to get a bed next to Dad. Ha—I'm hoping for a little bit more time with that one mate! You have to giggle—people say the funniest things…I should keep a book *Top 100 Things People Say to Someone with a Terminal Illness;* I hope you're all keeping up with these ideas…I'm determined to raise money for this 'grey area' and put something in place for the new Woking Hospice. Keep coming up with ideas, suggestions and connections, folks!

8 August 2014

P.S. Forgot to mention I have the mask! Thought my darling godson could go back to school with the best show and tell ever! Not before Dad tried it on to scare the nurses and Mum had a go!

9 August 2014

And the radiotherapy is finished! The effects will last for three weeks and my head is itchy beyond belief. Just need to rest and take things relatively slowly. I am seeing the doctor next week to talk about the chemo which will then start the following week. No rest for the wicked hey! My poor body, having to go through all of this again! I have so much stuff to do as well…paperwork mostly and getting all my bits in order. Not great when you have the energy levels of a flea. Saw the lovely Manolo yesterday at the hospice…he is very sweet and constantly checks on Dad, Mum and me. I hate to bring the conversation back to farts, but Manolo is a very honest man and is kind of on my case about sorting bits and bobs as well as my care plan for when the time comes. So much so that he makes me a little nervous as I kind of have to face the inevitable when he's around—no denying what the future holds with this one! This of course has resulted in a nervous tummy with the odd parp as he makes his way towards me. There's me denying the whole thing in my head and him like the white rabbit with a clock attached ticking away! I best get this bloody bucket list started I'm telling you!

On that note, I asked the oncologist today if I could holiday while on chemo…His answer was, "Lots." Dr Ralph is definitely my kind of man. When I asked him if I could drink on steroids, his answer was, "I think you might need one." Brilliant! Jo T went back again yesterday, boy were we sad to see her go. Poor girl has had to put up with more backside stories than ever, and this is a girl who hates these conversations! Offers of counselling back in Dubai for Jo would be most welcome and needed! Right, today my aim is to eat less and shrink the face! The docs have said I will lose weight…c'mon!

10 August 2014

22 days since diagnosis = madness! And I've already finished one round of treatment.

In those early hours of this morning, I found this: http://www.theguardian.com/…/…/top-five-.[11]

I want you to know that this was a good find! I don't have any of these regrets. I have followed all my dreams, have been an actress, teacher, worked abroad, been to some of the most amazing places in the world, travelled with some amazing

---

[11] Sally is referring to an article from the Guardian called 'Top five regrets of the dying' – this can still be looked up.

people, and have possibly the best friends ever—Fact, have the funniest family and generally have probably fulfilled most of my life's ambitions! There's still that bucket list to be having! Yes, I never had children and I ended up divorced, but looking back it's all for the best. I always had a fear of dying old, lonely and stinking of cat piss (I love cats) that's not going to happen now. I could have stayed in a miserable marriage and lost every ounce of my confidence—never experienced travelling and excuse the cliché but 'finding out who I was' as I did. You see, there are positives to everything and after reading that article I kind of feel lucky, in an ironic kind of way! I don't mean to sound callous, but the lady at the hospice when telling me what a breath of fresh air I was, told me about her mum dying and how miserable she had been for most of her life…it made me feel grateful for my life. Hope that makes sense.

There are two other things I wanted to share with you today: lots of you are like little researching bunnies out there—including you, Mum! For research purposes—I read and take on board all your advice btw—not had a cannabis cake yet Saz…there's still time! I have triple-negative advanced breast cancer. Slightly mental to read about, but it will give you some idea as to what might work, what doesn't and why the nasty critters may have been working their magic in my body. Just might help with future research materials!

Now my last sharing is caring about Dad. He makes me laugh on a daily basis! And the old man was so upbeat and positive yesterday; I have a feeling he may outlive me! When I told him this, he seemed particularly pleased with himself. Evelyn came and visited him yesterday all the way from Dubai and he recalled fondly all the wonderful restaurants, hotels and general giggles we'd had out there. Very precious moments indeed!

All in all, a good, positive day with no regrets! It's the small things in life and having no regrets is certainly up there.

11 August 2014

Hair falling out! Funniest part of this is watching it fly out at an Open-Air performance of 'Comedy of Errors!' Could have done with a glue stick! Never a pleasant experience losing the Barnet, especially when it's only just fully grown back.

New wig arriving today so fingers crossed, it looks ok and relatively normal! Kids are in for a shock in September! Now I have to master putting it on with one hand! Fingers crossed I manage this with one hand, and I have a feeling with the wind in the UK toupee tape is going to be a must! Don't really want to be chasing my syrup down the street!

1 August 2014

Keep wondering if writing the days down is a good or bad thing. I suppose the one thing it does do is keep some kind of bizarre order in my head to this mess I've got myself into! ATOTB, what is this? This week has been fab…Tiring, but fab, and it's allowed me to live a reasonably normal week. The whole-brain radiotherapy has been far scarier than any of the original breast cancer but working has kept that sense of normality. As before, I think that's important for my own well-being. I have made a conscious decision to rest next week though and finish this radiotherapy properly. I also want to spend as much quality time with Mum and Dad…this is time you can't get back, so it is the most important. My appetite is quite frankly doing my head in—I am starving Marvin 24/7 and although cutting the steroids to now one a day…I'm still bloody hungry!

It is probably my body's way of craving food, but seriously—moon face is a bloody understatement….as is a big fat tummy! I'm starting to seriously resemble White Dee from Benefits Street, I'm telling you! What with that and the fact I've not washed my hair this week for fear of it falling out! Am I painting a lovely picture for you all? I do need to sort this mind and next week I'm going to walk every day, which will help combat tiredness from the radiotherapy and keep me in good spirits. Last night Kerry came over and we spent a couple of hours with Dad laughing in the hospice about all sorts of things.

Me living in Dubai, him winding mum up…it was lovely. We showed him pics of Aya, and Anna, which he loved. It was just a lovely evening and the atmosphere in there was so calm and tranquil. Dad's temperature is still high and he daily fights infection. He was honest last night and told us that one of these bugs would eventually get him 'The bugs are gonna get me, mate', but we keep hoping this doesn't happen this week or indeed the next.

Cancer is such a horrible thing…eating away at people…just makes you wonder why it takes hold as it does and what Dad and I did wrong somewhere along the line! I blame my moon face, Betty Crocker and a love of bloody food! I jest! We're just a little bit unlucky I guess and there ain't a lot you can do about that. Have a good day folks…and eat your greens!

12 August 2014

This is definitely different from #100happydays but I am still trying to find positives in my day. So, the hair is falling out, there is no denying it—in bloody clumps, exactly as it did before! Jeesh I can't believe I have to go through this again! I remember standing at my front door sobbing my heart out on Wendy's shoulder only just short of three years ago and here we are again. This time mind I'm decidedly pissed off! In the car back up to Surbs it blew in Neil's face! In the hospice I got told off for pulling at it by the folks—there is something quite sadistic about doing that…and tonight, well it's coming out in handfuls! On the positive, it's lovely to be back in the flat, I had a lovely visit from Vickie, and have added to my bucket list—need to write this down and have come up with one charity idea, all good. So, in a need to remain positive…the following photos depict my recovery! Don't laugh at the new wig, it's being styled tomorrow. Neil actually nearly wet himself when I put this on straight out of the box!

And another positive…my hand has felt a little stronger today. Not full movement but definitely some—fingers, toes and anything else you can figure crossed please.

13 August 2014

Sitting on a bus going to hairdressers in a scarf and hat! Mortified!!! And yes, I felt like screaming that, hence the overuse of the exclamation! Those of you who know me well know that people's sympathy stares are driving me mad. I never want to look like the girl who has cancer, yet every wig I put on, scarf, hat, you name it…this morning pissed me off. My hair has come out so much now I look like one of the Witches in a Roald Dahl novel! Here's hoping John Mullan can weave his magic today! My darling dad took a turn for the worse yesterday. He continues to be very poorly and they were worried something might happen suddenly. He slept all day with Mum and me at his side…but oh yes; his cheekiness prevailed in the afternoon. The doctor (not his favourite of the two) was putting a cannula in as he was asleep. He didn't even flinch, but then I caught him open one eye and gave her a funny face when she wasn't looking, winked at me and then went back to his sick face! I swear my dad should have been a comedian…it was like a Benny Hill sketch!

Well, onwards and upwards, clearing the shed today with Alan, Andy and the dogs…lots of Stanley and Levi doggy love!

While I've been writing this, the bus has driven past a nasty accident at the end of my old road and an old person knocked off a bike! Count yourself lucky, Hitch…what's a few sympathy stares, hey?

14 August 2014

And I'm bloody bald, again! Who'd have thought it? Just as my hair was back to how it was pre-November 2011, it's gone again. My head is also sore this time (from the radiotherapy) and if it wasn't for some lovely friends yesterday who were around all day and joined by another gorgeous friend for a takeaway in the evening, I may well have had a hissy fit meltdown.

Sleeping seems to be eluding me at the moment with my favourite wake-up time being 4 a.m.! I really need more sleep than this. I think the head soreness does not agree with the pillow, hence waking me up…I need to find a way around this.

Anyhow, enough moaning for one morning. Dad was pretty chipper yesterday, phoning me up to give me instructions on cleaning my shed out. Alan, Andy and the dogs helped me all day with trips to the tip and cancer research shop (still optimistic about that miracle). Ironically, I looked for a top for four years in Dubai, only to find the blooming thing in the shed yesterday—ha! As well as some hilarious pics from the past! Sorry, I've gone off the subject, so back to Dad. His advice ended with him saying, "Get that bloody shed cleared and I don't want all your junk in my house! And you have all day as I'm not going to clop my pogs today." Hilarious…in the 44 years I've known my dad; he has been infamous for getting sayings wrong!

We've had many giggles over the years and today was another prime example. I can remember when I first had BC in 2011, Dad drove me to Maidstone for my first op saying, "If you need the loo, we have to stop in Crackit Lane services." Clacket, Dad…not Crackit! Ha! Mum and I were creased up in the car and it provided some light relief on a rather stressful morning!

So, today a trip to the hospice (wig-bravery or not…we shall see), followed by an appointment with my oncologist to discuss chemo for next week…the joys! I have also got to get down to some serious jobs, sorting, phone calls, Will, selling the car and a whole host of other stuff…lists Sally, lists!

Have a good day folks and girls—appreciate your hair, frizzy or not, be grateful you have it!

14 August 2014

Wiggage Day 1…Feeling a little brave but a little self-conscious too…convinced people are staring—to hell with it, they'd stare more if I popped it off. I've gone for the old faithful…bloody good job I didn't chuck them away, hey?

15 August 2014

A good day, Dad was in good form! I spent all afternoon with him; he slept for a long while and then woke up, chatted for England and was back to his hilarious, cheeky self. The nurses all come in and sit and chat with him too…He's a popular man is my dad, regaling stories of his Fuchsias and making everyone laugh with his cheekiness. He is determined to go to the London Fuchsia show on Sunday, just for an hour and the wheelchair, drip bag holders; cushions etc. are all ready. Fingers crossed his wish comes true on Sunday! I had an appointment with the oncologist yesterday regarding the chemo. Basically, I will stay on this chemo indefinitely, or until it stops working. It doesn't sound quite as harsh as the previous chemo I had, fingers crossed my body behaves and accepts the help generously. My hand is slowly returning to normal. I lack strength but can stretch my fingers and even do a poor man's jazz hand. Dr Ralph was really impressed with this and admitted he thought it might never come back. I am a determined girl though, been doing my exercises and have a Kill Bill attitude to it—thanks to Kerry Coburn for that one!

Anna Bishop, I have been told I'm going to lose weight! As we know this didn't happen last time, so result if it does! Got to be thankful for small things. Unbelievably my appetite has already decreased—good job!

Last night was horrible. Excruciating stomach pains and a bad tummy to go with it—boo! Feeling a little better this morning mind! I think half of the problem is the fact the doc has told me one of the side effects of the chemo is diarrhoea…this gives me the heeby jeebies after some stress-related IBS in the past and I fear the worrying has got the better of me—nervous poo's! Right…time to surface. Have a good day folks and I'll leave you with a pic of the improved hand!

16 August 2014

Can't believe where the summer hols are going! This is certainly one summer holiday I'm not going to forget! Especially as I missed out on some glorious acting work and choreographing a show for Edinburgh—gutted! Wishing you all going to Edinburgh an amazing time and if you're up there go and see Latymer Upper perform 'The Lawnchair Man' fabulous musical!

The hospice was madness yesterday—Dad is still his absolute cheeky self and lots of visitors…He is SO popular and I think he loves it!

I then had two amazing friends help me make a start on the paperwork! This is going to be a long job and one that's going to bring up lots of the past. I have some more v funny pics to post from my GSA days—keep a look out! It's amazing what a bit of sorting does though as for the first time in ages I slept like a baby…it must be therapeutic! As well as the sorting I laughed so hard last night that I nearly wet myself! Involuntary very loud farts from a very funny lady—you know who you are! And a discussion about piles! I have known these friends for 23 years and despite the gaps in seeing each other, we pick up where we left off every time. Yet again I sit feeling blessed to be lucky enough to have the most amazing people in my life.

Dad tried the wheelchair ready for Sunday yesterday and all seems good. We have a wheelchair taxi booked from the hospice at 10.30 a.m. and we're all still hopeful. Even if he manages half an hour, I know this will make Dad happy! I wonder what his next challenge will be. Maybe his garden at home. Without a doubt, he is getting smaller by the minute and more tired and Dad's diet consists of jelly and ice cream, with the occasional soup. Apparently, this is pretty normal with cancer patients—not quite sure I'm looking forward to that!

Right, more washing and sorting for me! Have a good one folks!

17 August 2014

Sorry for the delay! Sadly, Dad didn't make the flower show today. Thanks for all your positive thoughts and wishes. He practiced in the wheelchair yesterday for about 20 minutes and it totally exhausted him to the point he slept for the rest of the day. I was more than a little worried last night but in true Hitch style, Dad called at 6.45 this morning to say he felt better…Was making us laugh today and both he and Neil Broughton took the piss out of my wig, saying that I had a rat on my head and it was moving! The pair of them thought they were hilarious! Bloody cheek!

Apart from an itchy head from the radiotherapy and the wiggage I seem to be getting my energy back (well I did fall asleep in the hospice and snored), but I got up this morning, made Dad banana cake, did some washing and even managed to pack my overnight bag. The hand is still weak, but I can do so much more with it—including doing up my bra again—hoorah!

So, things are still good and the Hitch family are still smiling—kind of!

Big thanks to Mel and the Hammonds for helping me yesterday and Neil for running me around like a nuttier today and tomorrow. Pelvic scan tomorrow…Would be nice to have some good news on this—if the cancer is there too, well, I'll cope! Let's hope not though.

18 August 2014

Just a quick one today: scan was good! Just a cyst on the ovaries, very normal and no nasty bits on it, so they'll check it every three to six months…Hoorah! She actually told me all was rather good down there considering I've been through cancer once plus the fact that chemo has a tendency to make everything go a bit funny!

20 August 2014

Sleep has eluded me again. I can't complain, had a good seven hours the night before and I think the nervousness of the chemo today has got the better of me. To say I'm shitting myself is, to put it mildly. I have no idea what effect this chemo will have on me as I don't know anyone who's been on it. The side effects include sore palms and feet. I've been advised to get 'udderly' cream for this, a loose tummy (terrific and not great for tube to school), possible nausea and the obligatory loss of taste. Dr Ralph said most people suffer with the first two…We shall see! Oh! And mouth ulcers too! I remember this feeling of anticipation last time I had chemo…it's hard to predict how your body will cope. Last time I knew it had to get through six cycles though and then it would be over! This chemo will carry on until it stops working! Saying that—there is a woman who has completed 160 cycles of it whom Dr Ralph thinks I should meet!

They keep telling me I will lose weight…bloody good job after the amount of cake I consumed yesterday! Not ideal on any level…I should be avoiding sugar at all costs…mini meltdown methinks!

Yesterday was filled with long-distance buddies who I miss incredibly! Adele Minter-Bradley chauffeured me around all day and supported me with Mum while I finally filled out my 'death plan'. Sounds like something out of Star Wars! I have finally realised the positive of this—it's done and now I can get on with my life knowing my wishes and requests will be followed…I must remember to write down the fact that when the time comes the Manolo Blahnik's need to go on! I'm not even kidding you. My feet better not swell, I'm telling you all now!

Dad is still in good form. His appetite is slowly coming back which is great as his strength will get better. I tell you— this man has the constitution of an Ox! One minute we are worried sick, the next he is severely taking the piss out of us! Don't get me wrong, he is an incredibly ill man still but he never fails to surprise us!

Last night was wonderful to catch up with Sam, Dawn and Arthur. My how this little boy has grown and how funny he is! A lot of my Dubai buddies are flying home this week. It's been so lovely having them around. They were my support network last time I went through this and I know there are times I'm going to miss them incredibly! Thank god for Skype!

I feel blessed to have amazing buddies all over the world and know my Brit Buddies are here and secretly glad I'm home this time!

Right—I've waffled enough. Am still mulling some favourite ideas around regarding charity stuff and know we'll get there eventually. Am thinking I could actually attend the first event! That's quite an exciting prospect and something else to get my teeth into. The bucket list is also slowly growing, and Manolo's face was a picture when I told him I would be spending Christmas in New York! Emma Victoria Barnes and Sarah Roberts Oshea need to see if I can get medical insurance for a week.

Have a lovely day…positive vibes for the first chemo cycle.

21 August 2014

I think I'm going to like the Nuffield in Guildford! The nurses were just lovely and at last I have a breast cancer nurse who is super! This is the thing Dubai doesn't do particularly well. I was damn lucky to have so many friends as the support care is not quite as good. There is also a group based there called 'Secondary Sisters', not quite sure about the name, but at long last it will give me the opportunity to talk to other people with advanced breast cancer.

I walked away with the biggest bag of drugs and herein is my life for the foreseeable future. Four chemo drugs twice a day with food. The first lot went in after supper last night and stayed down. Bar the narcolepsy taking over—I was like a nodding dog on the sofa—I feel ok! I'm a bit if a wimp and have never really liked popping pills—just going to have to suck this one up and see. I have sickness tablets and diarrhoea tablets to take if necessary (too much info, but you so know I'm going to share it anyhow).

Dad had a little blip yesterday. His kidneys are not working too well and the honesty from the doctor about surviving an op made him a little sad. There is one thing we know…Dad does not want to die in St Peter's. Life is a funny old thing and facing your own mortality is filled with fear, crying and giggles! I keep banging on but I'm telling you…this is the best TV idea out there. When the giggles come and the humour is dark, you've never heard anything like it!

Right…a lie-in for me this morning—bliss! Breakfast and chemo tablets now! Fingers crossed this chemo suits me and prolongs my life to annoy you for much longer.

26 August 2014

It's been a hard few days and I needed a little quiet time. My darling dad passed away on 22 August. He was sleeping peacefully and in no pain and as hard as it was, we knew how sick Dad was. I feel blessed to have had a little over a month with him to 'chew the fat' about living with cancer. I wish in some ways I'd asked him a lot more!

I think it's fair to say that this awful disease takes too many lives, too early. Unfortunately, watching it take someone who means the world to you brings everything that little closer to home. I don't mind telling you all I'm bloody petrified, to say the least, and over the last few days I've tried very hard to remain positive and upbeat about my own diagnosis…slightly selfish really with everything going on, but I'm sure Dad would be telling me to look after myself!

The good news is the chemo seems to be ok. I stupidly read some stuff on the Internet about side effects and wished I hadn't…Bar my appetite dropping (believe me, after the steroid munching this is no bad thing), I seem to be ok. I'm not quite a week in yet, so we'll see. I'm on oral chemo this time, two weeks of tablets and then a rest week, followed by the whole process again. This first load will give me some idea as to how I feel at what points in the cycle which will then make it easier to plan things and cope with work. Btw School have been amazing and totally supportive!

This week will be a busy one with Dad's funeral to arrange and lots of paperwork. I suppose it's going to be a difficult one. But hopefully, we'll draw strength on the good times. We have some amazing memories of him and we will continue to celebrate his life.

27 August 2014

Well, yesterday was a day filled with things that needed doing. Paperwork at home followed by the difficult task of planning my lovely dad's funeral. Years ago, my dad and his brother worked at Woking Crematorium…they used to come home and relay stories about what actually happened there. This was not particularly helpful yesterday as the lovely funeral director talked us through the committal and the smooth transition of the body. My mum and I both started giggling rather inappropriately and then had to explain ourselves. We know, you see, that there's someone behind turning the wheel. I just know Dad was with us giggling yesterday and all the decisions we made were influenced by him. We even suggested a BOGOF![12] Thank goodness the lady had a similar sense of humour!

I feel lucky we had that time with Dad to ask him what he wanted. It did make yesterday much easier. It also made me think about my own funeral, not in a miserable way but rather quite a positive one. For someone who is incredibly fussy, it does mean I choose things that I want. Don't get me wrong...I kind of shit myself (metaphorically at the moment but could be a chemo side effect later down the line) at the thought, but hey...there is one thing we are all certain of in life—sadly we're going to pass at some point. What would be the point of living if we didn't know this? The only difference is that I've been forewarned that mine will come sooner. I suppose I've been given a little look into the future. That sounds terribly morbid, doesn't it? I promise you, I do actually see this as a positive.

There is one thing I'm not enjoying this time round and that's the wig! How can it be more comfortable to wear a wig in Dubai than in the UK? Air conditioning, my friends! I constantly want to whip the bloody thing off but fear I may be seen as the 'Surbiton Mad Woman!'

28 August 2014

I dreamt my hair came back! Sure, it was thin etc., but it came back and if I popped it into a ponytail and had the front straight, it hid the thin bits! And it was blonde again! I'm wondering if I'm the only baldie who has these dreams. Alan Bradshaw Neil Broughton and the rest of my fellow hairless buddies, over to you?

---

[12] By one get one free.

I managed a short yoga session yesterday which was just lovely! Stretching and breathing…I think we all forget to breathe sometimes and I can't even begin to tell you how much better I felt afterwards. My buddy (yep he's my fellow baldie too) Alan continually leaves me the following mantra on my phone 'shoulders back, head high and don't forget to breathe' it's such a good thing to remember!

Massive, massive thank you to those who have donated to the Woking Hospice in celebration of Dad. Overwhelmed by people's generosity is an understatement! We are still going to create a special charity and ideas are flowing. And I'm at that first event—I'm telling you now.

Today we are meeting the vicar to discuss the order of service…Tina Turner is in their Dad…I promise you!

Have a good day folks…and don't forget to breathe.

31 August 2014

Today, if it weren't for the wig I'd feel bloody brilliant! Had the best night at 'Tumble' thank you, Ashley Vallance, and had some cool selfies…well they might have been if I wasn't wearing a bloody wig and looking like Thelma from Scooby-Doo! Anyhow, here's the selfies for giggles…Alan Bradshaw, Peter Duncan sends his love! Sarah, Kerry sends her love! Paul Jones so near, yet so far! I so could have come and sat with you. Just to let you all know…I am so not impressed with wig/outfit look! Please do not tell me otherwise! It didn't spoil a good evening though and H was bloody amazing!

1 September 2014

It's been busy...organising and preparing bits for my lovely dad's funeral and then back to school this morning, albeit briefly! Thanks, Vickie for letting me stay last night, made a huge difference to the getup!

My work buddies are just out of this world. It was brilliant to see them all this morning and the support was overwhelming, thanks guys!

So, Secondary Sisters was actually alright! There I was, making everyone laugh and encouraging people to remain positive! I think they'll have me back again! A mixed group of ages, I think I was the youngest, everyone was welcoming and it was quite a giggle. Also left with a massive bag of make-up and skin care products so bonus! The bottom line is it's good to talk to other people who have been given the cancer sentence! The brain tumour issue still freaks me out as everyone is most frightened of this! It's that fart-releasing moment when people say 'they thought it had gone to my brain but thank goodness it hasn't' paaaarrrrrp! Best get this fundraising event up and running if I want to attend!

Wednesday is the last day of chemo and then a week off...This means cycle one is complete—yay! As I've said, I'll be on this till it stops working. I just hope my hair comes back! On that note, if you watched Eastenders—how the hell has Carol's hair grown back in a few weeks? I think they need to employ me.

I've got an ice bucket challenge to do at some point—thanks, Mel! I think it's going to have to be 'special!'

9 September 2014

It's been a hard few weeks, hence the tardiness. Dad's funeral was a wonderful send-off to a wonderful man. There are days when I think of him with a smile on my face and days when I miss him and realise I'm not going to speak to him again—they are the hardest ones.

Today though was a good one and a return to normality. After what I can only describe as eight weeks of pure shit, I went back to work and despite my worries yesterday, it was fine. Kids are an amazing cure—you have no time in a lesson to think about yourself. I like that. It also helps that I work with some of the most amazing people who have been just wonderfully supportive, taking lessons from me and generally making life bearable, allowing me to carry on. I truly have been blessed with amazing work friends both in Dubai when I was first diagnosed and here. I continue to say it, I am lucky to have friends like this.

Saturday was a fab night at Guys and Dolls seeing little Nic do his stuff and then a great night with the girls afterwards. Despite the fact the wig makes me hotter than a very hot thing and that I'm slightly worried about pissed people and their flailing cigarettes: 'highly flammable people', for a few hours I didn't feel like there was anything wrong with me.

So, now…attention to detail. Paperwork to sort, stuff to apply for and a bucket list to write down and start to tick things from. Dinner at the Shard in Designer Shoes being the top of the list and the date in the diary is booked for next week. I don't know how long I have, but Dad made me promise him I wouldn't put things off and I would get on with it! I'm on a mission…

16 September 2014

Day 58 (that's quite a long time since diagnosis now).

Work, theatre, friends…life is good and slowly the bucket list is coming together. There's even been a few things suggested that I've already done…Tick! All I need now is to stay strong and healthy enough to get my arse over to Australia and New Zealand in 2015.

The chemo is ok at the moment which is a relief, although the oncologist wants to up the next dose…I am supposed to see how much my body can take and to keep shrinking the critters! I won't know how well everything is working until they scan me, which should happen after the next round of drugs. I feel good so hopefully that's a good sign. I have an annoying little cough which of course makes me paranoid, but I'm sure if they'd never told me the cancer had made tiny spots on my lungs I wouldn't have developed the cough. The mind plays funny tricks!

I miss my dad. I miss his humour and his advice, especially with so much going on and putting the flat on the market etc. He told me not to put anything off though and to do all the things I want to while I'm well, and this is the mantra I'm carrying around with me right now!

The wig? Well, I don't mind telling you that this pisses me off on a daily basis. Dubai is certainly a more wig-friendly place. There is now the worry of getting said wig stuck in tube doors, pulled off by low-hanging tree branches, blown off by gusts of wind (not mine I hasten to add) and caught in my rucksack! Ermmmm panic! That's without the smoke brigade waving their fags around in the streets! I am doing a lot of ducking and holding the top like a hat! The taupe tape might have to come out soon…not brill! I'm sure Carol Jackson on

Eastenders never has these problems! The relief when I get home and take the bloody thing off is amazing! I was going to say something else then but deleted it! I'll let you guess! Oh, one last thing…thank you! You are a pretty amazing bunch of people!

17 September 2014

Blimey 60 whole days since I was admitted to the hospital into the ward next door to my darling dad with a dodgy hand! Certainly didn't see what was to come on that day! So, the flat is getting there and Neil has started the inside repairs on the window and wall from all the rain we had at the beginning of the year! A few more bits and bobs and it's ready for the market. In all honesty, it's been a funny day. *I felt not myself this morning…knackered* I think, *which has made me realise that I do need to make sure I factor in rest and get my seven to eight hours in.* As a good friend quotes me from 'A Fault in Their Stars', *sleep kills cancer…*I reckon there's some truth in there! I also today started the task of clearing and doing jobs that I've put off. I can understand why, it's bloody difficult throwing things away that ordinarily you'd keep. I'm not making sense, but basically, when you know you have a future, these things might be useful and can often play a part in that future. For me today, there wasn't that pull and in turn, it made me again have to face what the future holds.

Gosh, I'm really not trying to be morbid here, you know me, but rather truthful and to give you some insight into the little things I feel occasionally. Inevitably as well today, with Neil working on the flat there was a little voice missing, telling us what to do. I think somehow my dad wriggled his humour into Neil and there was plenty of piss-taking and banter going on about my baldie head, so in some ways, it felt like my dad was with us. A walk in Richmond Park this afternoon seemed to blow those cobwebs away and a few trips down memory lane, revisiting my old Halls of Residence and our old flat in Putney. God that was a lovely road!

On a more upbeat note, it would seem that Christmas is going to be really special! Not only spending it in New York with mum but with Emma Victoria Barnes and her mum too and if we're really lucky the third one too…! Two of my bestest buddies! It's been ten years since the three of us were all together and that was at my wedding! I'm saying nothing more on the subject!

I am so excited for the weekend to do my first bucket list activity! A few people have suggested I post the list here so if you fancy joining me on any of these activities you can! What do you reckon? Right…eight hours sleep and I've blown it already updating the blog all good plans! I'll leave you with a pic of a little fella (actually could well be a girl, not up on deers) who seemed a little like me today. Following his path warily and treading carefully unsure of his future. Lots of love and sleep tight!

20 September 2014

I feel hair! I can actually feel hair at the front of my head—yep it's definitely there…little prickly spikes! Oh please start growing…I know you can do it, you've done it before! And on that exciting note…I am about to accomplish one of the first things on my bucket list this evening…the list is still currently in my head, but I promise to write and share it soon. Now to just rid myself of this niggling nausea and things will be good and before you suggest it…anti-nausea tablets or wine this evening? I know which I'm choosing—naughty Hitch! Xx

21 September 2014

Washing my hair has taken on a whole new level! Thought it might give you a giggle!

At the Shard London!

So, there are a few things in London on my bucket list (still not written but in my head—I will get on with it, I promise). Anyhow…I have been to the OXO Tower many times before, I love it there, and the views, the atmosphere etc., but never have I come out of the lift and turned left into the restaurant. Don't get me wrong, the brasserie is wonderful, but the restaurant…now that's something else. The food was to die for, the wine—perfect and the service was perfection. On top of this, we had an amazing table by the window with views of St Paul's. I went with my friend Vickie from Latymer, who along with my boss Justin, have become amazing friends and just like you Dubai folk, they are helping to make my life as normal as it can possibly be right now—something I will be eternally grateful for. I digress, so yes, I think we used the cancer to our advantage last night! And why the hell not, it's not every day you're doing things off your bucket list because you actually know your death date's been brought forward! We even went full out and had taxis last night…I think this is definitely the way to a successful night in London!

After the amazing OXO Tower, we got a taxi to the Shard. I thought we were going to the bar in Aqua Shard and was quite happily walking in when Vickie announced we needed to get another lift. What! Oh the 'Vicster' had a little surprise up her sleeve. Like a dog with a bone, when there were no tables available in the Shangri-La bars, she wrote to the manager, explained the circumstances and boom, a table in the window was made available for us with complimentary champagne. Not only that, the manager herself came and took us on a tour of the hotel and restaurants and showed us the best views. I even regaled the story of Mum and Dad being on the viewing platform of the Burj Khalifa watching Tom Cruise hanging off the side! Mission Impossible was being filmed and the pair of them were convinced it was his stunt double, until the close-up pic that Mum took revealed it was actually the man himself! Can't wait till they film him swinging from the Shard!

Now I've been a lucky girl and have been to some of the most amazing hotels in the world, but yesterday…to be sat in a bar on the 52nd floor of the Shard in my beloved London, the best city in the world! Well, you just can't beat that! Yesterday was awesome (Americans do adjectives well hey?). So, two items on the bucket list with a big fat tick next to them. Is it wrong to think I'm going to quit like this year? What's the saying? *If life deals you lemons—make gin and tonic!*

28 September 2014

What a busy, busy week it's been. Seeing lots of lovely people for dinner, an evening at the ballet with one of my dearest buddies and seeing one of my ex-pupils take one of the leads—boy is she an amazing dancer! And then today at the Malvern horticultural show with my mum and godmother. Both the fuchsia that were cultivated for Dad in his memory; 'John Hitchcock' and 'Johnny Boy' were at the show, but due to it being the end of the season, they were lacking flowers. Hence, it's been decided, that these will be launched at Hampton Court Flower Show, the show that Dad was so desperate to go to this year, an outing that illness robbed him of.

This is also a little bit of added pressure on me…I certainly need to keep myself going till then and also for a dear friend who just got engaged and is getting married in August—come on, Hitch, you can do this! Well, I bloody hope so. Lovely Manolo, my palliative care nurse (who I genuinely like a lot but who makes me emit little farts with his honesty), told me I probably had months rather than years. My reaction was a picture, "WTF Manolo…are you bloody kidding me?"

"Well, months can go into double figures, Sally, like 24 months," I tell you, that man is hilarious. I can't imagine what he says to his girlfriend…"Does this make me look fat, Manolo?"

"Darling, it's not the clothes that make you look fat; shall I make us a cup of tea?" I shouldn't be cruel, I genuinely do like Manolo and I think he can read me like a book, hence he knows we can have honest conversations. I also like the way I can react to Manolo and he takes it and giggles with me.

Being busy this last week has been wonderful but it's definitely taken its toll on my body and in turn, I'm a tired girl. *Sleep kills cancer!* I also seemed to have developed every side effect going from the chemo. Sore feet, diarrhoea like you've never witnessed (sorry for the graphic description, but seriously…I live in a one-bedroom flat!) and on top of all of this another big fat period (I'm supposed to be going through my menopause—something I was so thrilled didn't happen last time but this time, hey it's not such an issue), and a bloody cough! I worry about getting the tube to work in the mornings, so many people coughing and sneezing, the germs must be flying around in these carriages! I will talk to my oncologist about the cough on Wednesday, but I hope to god that it is merely a common cough! Ever since they told me I had tumours on my lungs, I developed a nervous cough…ridiculous, and I felt absolutely fine before I knew this.

There have been some rather exciting developments as well over the past couple of weeks, now is not the right time to discuss them but watch this space. This bubbling excitement could well mean that I can start my campaign to put free TVs back in NHS hospitals. I feel so strongly that if my dad had experienced some stimulus in the hospital, however mindless, just a bit of background noise to see the world was still going on, it would have made a massive difference to his time there. It still sends shivers down my spine to remember how 'browned off' and upset he was. I feel sure free TVs in hospitals are the way forward.

Right…I was ready for bed at 8.30 p.m. and it's now 10.30 p.m. Bedtime for me. I'm off to see Kylie tomorrow at the O2, oh yeah—thank you so much, Carolyn Saul, I think/know the Hitch girls are going to have a ball with you!

Goodnight lovely people and use hand sanitiser on public transport…just saying!

3 October 2014

It's been a hectic week and although I've spent a lot of it not feeling very well with a cough and seem to have lost my appetite (not so worrying—plenty of timber left); the week has been exciting and I'm kind of pinching myself with support and opportunities that are coming my way. Maybe some good will come out of all of this after all!

Tonight was the most special of nights. Surprising little Lana with dinner in Covent Garden and then presenting her with a golden ticket to the restaurant to let her know she was having an early birthday present to see Charlie and the Chocolate Factory. Her little face was an absolute picture…I can't even begin to tell you.

These kinds of evenings are fun and exciting (I'll be honest, Charlie and the Chocolate Factory was on the bucket list…tick), but these lovely days out are a little tainted with the question: will this be the last birthday I see of Lana's? I'm hoping not, but it is there, in the back of my mind…and I want to relish every moment I possibly can.

When I split up with Ab, I spent most Saturdays with Cate, Rick and Lana watching Dancing on Ice with Bonnie Langford and the like. They became my weekends when I was too busy feeling sorry for myself to live my life and get out there and meet someone else. I always wonder if boys find this easier than girls—to get back out there. What a waste, 36 and I thought I was too old. I moped for far too long. I regret that so much now…I was young, I should have relished every minute of it with my then-healthy body. Anyhow, I digress—Lana used to climb onto my lap and give me a big hug and then later named me Her Sally. She's a budding little dancer—that's how her mum, Cate and I met, studying dance at university. It's so lovely to see her blossom and I'm sure she will achieve great, great things! She sat and told me this evening everything about the audition process for Charlie and the Chocolate Factory; she obviously has her sights set high.

I wish to god I was going to see all these wonderful things I know she will achieve.

I've said before, that the only regret I have is not having children. I have some of the most wonderful kids in my life, thanks to my gorgeous friends who allow me to be part of their lives. A godson who shares my love of musical theatre (he wants to go to Wicked—I'm coming again, Rowley), and he also shares my naughty sense of humour. He can make me laugh at the drop of a hat and we only have to look at each other to know what the other is thinking. Yes, I don't have children, but I've been blessed with many gorgeous children, including two who call me Aunty Silly! I have no idea why!

Anyway, enough of the sadness, I want to tell you about my tube journeys to work at the moment. First of all, I have a wig on! That is hot...Not in a sexy way before you misread but in a furnace way! I always try and get a seat on the tube as I do get tired (apparently this is still from the radiotherapy). I sometimes get a guilty look...Tube commuters are good at this, they pull this sad forlorn 'I'm having a really bad day' face and expect you to give up your seat. It's ok if you're pregnant as you wear a badge now saying 'baby on board'. Well, worry no more, Hitch, as I bring you the 'Cancer on Board' badge. That'll shut all you miserable commuters up. I know it's blunt...made me giggle though! I also realised today as I walked up the stairs in Wimbledon that you practically walk with your head in someone else's backside! Jeesh, there was a man with a big bottom this morning in front of me, I didn't breathe...Just in case! I'm also feeling slightly guilty about the odd guff I might have emitted on that staircase in the last year—oops!

I've waffled enough. Today has been a lovely day and with some very special news from a lovely couple. Apologies now for sobbing at your good news, but I can't wait to meet another little lady who I wish I could see grow up to be as absolutely special as her mummy and daddy!

Sleep tight folks, it is way past my bedtime!

There is no life I know
To compare with pure imagination
Living there, you'll be free
If you truly wish to be, I'm off to dream…

5 October 2014

Blogging in bed—not sure it's the best thing to do before going to sleep, but was desperate to get a couple of things down!

I'd like to say a massive thank you to everyone for checking out the article in the *Mail* on Sunday today. I know it was difficult for some of you to pick that particular paper up! It is the start though of raising awareness of bringing back 'Free TVs in National Health Hospitals'. There are other avenues we are exploring and I want to raise money for this, cancer charities and hospices.

This weekend has been just what the doctor ordered. Lots of rest! I put my phone on silent yesterday and did nothing, but watch rubbish (I love it) TV. I will get back to you all I promise but am getting a little overwhelmed trying to fit everything in. I've also had problems with my appetite and the thought of eating out right now is not brilliant. Saying that I had a lovely lunch at my boss Justin's house today. Thank you, Fran…you made yummy food that my stomach was happy to consume—miracle worker! My friend Vickie has suggested that maybe I'm better at eating with others. She may well be right. At the end of the day, the thought of cooking makes me feel queasy. I know…I need a chef.

As it was late and it was a Sunday (meaning the buses are few and far between) when I got back to Surbiton this evening, I got a cab home. Laziness personified! Anyhow, the taxi driver and I got into a big conversation about the glorious weather. We ate dinner outside today at Justin's, it was lovely! We then moved on to the debate about global warming…to which the taxi driver stated, "We're all going to die next year"…no shit, Sherlock…bloody hell, I stepped into the grim Reapers cab this evening, I'm telling you. Be thankful I'm up penning this! I survived the black cab horror.

We played a fab game today…I need Vickie Bedford to remind me of the name, but knowing how you all have a bit of a dark sense of humour, you'll love it! Will fill you in when I find out, but when I tell you one of the answers was, "Shitting in Pudsey's missing eye socket," you will understand this is not a game for children.

Sleep tight folks…hope my dad would have been proud today of the little article and picture.

8 October 2014

So, today…Inspired by several enthusiastic and amazing people, I have well and truly started my campaign to raise money for free TVs in NHS Hospitals. I have written St Peter's Hospital an email and I have pledged to put free TVs in all their side rooms. If we start small, with one hospital, hopefully, we can get further recognition and get free TVs in all NHS hospitals. I'm actually, incredibly excited. There are amazing ideas flying around from some amazingly, clever and caring people and I'm sure we can do this and make a difference to peoples' quality of life when they are incredibly ill in hospital. So…this is what you can do, if you have, or know anyone with a spare TV, or you're getting a new one…

Please, please, please save your TVs while I work out what we do next. If anyone has any contacts at St Peter's who might be able to help me further, I would be very grateful. Always good to have a foot in the door. Have felt bloody rubbish again today and cancelled my appointments with Manolo and my counsellor…yep, I've decided to see a counsellor. I figure it's good to chat and I need some 'me time' to try and make sense of all this shit that's engulfing my life right now. She's a lovely lady, Spanish and totally behind me making it to the Tomatina Festival next year. I will probably have to wear a helmet as a blow to the head might be a little dangerous but it's on that bucket list! Sadly, I was too late for it this year. Anyway, after convincing my friend Wendy that I was fine and she didn't need to come up, she ignored me anyhow and arrived with flowers, champagne and a choice of nausea-friendly foods (well I'm trying them and I'll let you know the best). Fizzy elderflower was good and made me belch which I think helped. What friendship hey! I even tried to call her in the car, but Wendy knew me too well and just ignored my call! I can't tell you, how an hour of giggling and a little walk in the park opposite (even with a scarf on my head) made me feel better.

If I could get rid of this nausea, I think I'd be fine…maybe I should just succumb to the anti-sickness tablets and in turn, hope that sorts my taste. It's a good job I have timber on me I tell you, had I been a skinny girl I'd be in serious trouble right now! I've also had the dreaded toilet problems today as well...my poor toilet; I only cleaned it this weekend. I had a funny thought today...I was trying not to strain (too much info) but I couldn't help thinking, that this could be a disaster...I could actually die on the bog, imagine the poor person who finds me! I know it's not funny, but it is a little and, in all honesty, I love toilet humour! Sally Hitchcock— died on the bog having a crap! It'd be a funny swan song!

Right...time to attempt to eat something to take the chemo tablets with. If you suggest to me a big meal right now, it's probably not going to go down too well, so apologies for that. It's small and picking right now...hopefully, it'll change...maybe this time I will lose the weight. Serves me right, last time, I remember laughing to Anna Bishop that I was going to lose weight! I bloody put it on! This chemo has a totally different effect, I think even my moonfaced is shrinking. I am also sleeping nine to ten hours a night...longer than ever in my life!

Happy British Bake Off watching folks and dare I say it TOWIE!

14 October 2014

Ok, this is my statement on my FB page! Tonight was up there on the bucket list! Seeing the one show I have always wanted to see revived, followed by meeting one of my idols and comparing notes on the role! And catching up with Andrew Reed, meeting his lovely brother, catching up with Vickie Jukes and her hubby...all thanks to two wonderful friends Kathryn Rooney and Michael Harrison! Gypsy, my friends, was bloody brilliant! Thank you, Roons, for making tonight possible for both Mum and I. Love you loads, xxxx, I can't even begin to tell you how bloody privileged and lucky I am to have seen this show…my favourite show of all time in my lifetime! Everything happens for a reason folks and thank goodness this was revived now and not in a couple of years! There are days when you forget you're ill and can't believe how incredibly lucky you are—today is one of those days! Night folks.

19 October 2014

*wig in the bath pic…and here she is again, having a little wash in readiness for Dubai! Am rather wondering if my hair doesn't grow back and whether she'll last…there were a few hairs coming out tonight with the knots! So wiggy friends…am I earning my stripes do you think?

Waking up ridiculously early after going to bed really late can only mean one thing…hangover! I may have lost my appetite, but I seem to be able to quaff the champagne still! It must be the bubbles! What a wonderful party last night was for Paul Jones's 40th birthday! Fabulous dancing, gambling and a marquee full of gorgeous people which is a credit to what bloody wonderful people you and Stephen are! It was also wonderful to see Mum let her hair down, dancing away and being a little social butterfly. Makes me happy to see her like this and know she'll be fine. Now the fact that as I'm writing this she's just gone to the loo with the bloody door open (my mum's house is a bungalow) is not so impressive—'shut the bloody door!' Jeesh, a week in Dubai sharing a room is going to prove interesting, that's for sure!

The wig went down well last night. Loads of people say they can't believe it's a wig—I think they probably say that to make me feel better…All the same, I'll take the compliment. And I also feel a bit of a fake as everyone tells me how well I look. I'm a dab hand with slapping the war paint on and losing a bit of timber, due to the appetite dip, hasn't done me any harm—at least my clothes fit me again after my eating machine steroid experience—I never realised my face could get that big! I don't want to go on steroids again, that's a fact! I'd never fit my face in the bloody coffin for a start! Stephen's niece did an amazing fire-eating display last night-totally out of this world! Was a little close to the start though and when a big fireball came, I had to run for cover—it may look real but I keep telling you people—highly flammable materials on my head! Maybe I should be wearing a warning badge or something.

Today would have been Mum and Dad's 51st wedding anniversary. This time last year I organised a surprise party for the two of them to celebrate. In all fairness, Dad was not 100 per cent, but it was a great night spent with all their family (that'll be mine as well then) and friends. I went home with a torn hamstring trying to demonstrate to my godson and little Lana that I could still do the splits! Epic fail Hitchcock! You had enough bloody trouble doing the splits at 10! Never was particularly supple—should have stretched more! Anyhow, today we're going to have a nice lunch at The White Heart and raise a little glass to my lovely dad! And then…damn, I need to pack! Hospital Monday, work Tuesday and fly Wednesday to Dubai. Bring me sunshine! I can't wait to see my Dubai buddies and have a good catch-up. I will mostly be at The Crowne Plaza in the pool, lying on a comfy sun bed or in the spa…feel free to pop in. Gloat, me? Yeah, why not…I'm going to enjoy every minute of these coming months! All the time I'm well enough I intend to relish every moment! Right, let's try and sleep this hangover off! Shit! How long does alcohol stay in your blood for? I've got my blood tests tomorrow! Oooops!

20 October 2014—Day 93 since diagnosis!

Who'd have thought 93 days have passed? Actually, in all honesty, it feels like I had that news ages ago!

Well, today has been a funny old day. I spent this morning at the hospital having my blood and collecting my chemo ready for Wednesday—I'll have to take the first lot on the plane over to Dubai…best not to drop those then!

Getting to the hospital early and seeing the sad news that Lynda Bellingham had sadly died kind of put me in an uneasy frame of mind, which as you know is quite unlike me. I've followed her story and her decision to stop the chemo with lots of interest, (not that I have any intention of giving up chemo right now). We also have the writing thing in common, so that's been something else I've been quite fascinated by. To see her pass so quickly after stopping the chemo is slightly frightening, to say the least. There was also the story of a young girl on 'Stand Up 2 Cancer' on Friday night, she really focused and positive in her attitude and reminded me a lot of myself. The titles that came up after her interview saying she had passed away were like a blow to the stomach…a little like my reaction this morning. I feel like I'm enjoying my life so much at the moment and totally forget that I'm ill and then wham…it hits you—shit (sorry mum), I am actually sick, I forgot!

Well in true Hitch style, this feeling soon went. Spending the morning in the hospital with Neil couldn't really have been a better cure. A morning of piss-taking, me seriously not being able to do one answer in The Times crossword (god I'm thick) and plenty of banter soon took my mind off everything. A trip to Sainsbury's and my scarf flying off was yet another reason for laughter…Not mine I hasten to add. I was in a mild panic shouting, "Help me with the knot," and Neil bent over pissing himself. Serves me right…I had literally just been being cocky in the car!

Lauren (lovely oncology nurse) thought Neil was my dad this morning. The poor woman walked in and said is your dad coming in, then realised that dad had died, then got totally flustered and apologetic and begged me not to a) tell Neil and b) said she hadn't looked at him properly! Loved relaying this one to him…no wonder he laughed when the scarf blew off! Best wear some toupee tape tomorrow methinks…there's a storm coming.

I've done lots of paperwork this afternoon; always makes you feel better and now time to pack! Work tomorrow and then I'm off on my hols—can't wait to see my Dubai buddies and to have a fruit beer on Thurs night; for someone with no appetite, I have a bit of a taste for fruit beer. I'm quite sure there'll be some funny stories to relay—remember I'm sharing a room with Mum! Earplugs—thanks for reminding me!

4 November 2014

That means I've got through 109 days…a pretty mean feat I reckon, 109 days and I'm still going and on the whole feeling pretty chipper. I looked in my diary yesterday as I wanted to know the date I had this awful diagnosis—you wouldn't believe it—St Swithin's Day. Have you read *One Day*? A lovely friend recommended it to me when I was first diagnosed in 2011, and I avidly read it, a beautiful but emotional book set around St Swithin's Day. How apt and what a good way to remember the diagnosis date. Here's hoping I'll be celebrating St Swinthin's Day next year with you all!

So, Mum and I had a lovely time in Dubai. Plenty of rest and relaxation and filled with wonderful friends, love and kindness. Having Sarah with us for the first weekend was an added bonus and it's the first time I've found saying goodbye hard. I feel blessed to have friends all over the globe and the goodbyes get harder each time. The appetite was shocking in Dubai and still carries on. Don't get me wrong, the weight loss is marvellous; I can now fit into everything and feel great. Let's hope it evens out though as I worry I'm not getting all the nutrients I need into me, although cucumbers and bananas are still up there and no, that's not a euphemism!

Today is a big day for me as it's my first scan since initially being in hospital on 15 July (sorry, I've well and truly put St Swithin's Day in your mind now, you'll hate me for that in years to come, or maybe you'll pick a little flower for me and have a happy moment). A full body CT scan to see if these critters are behaving themselves. I was supposed to have a bone scan which was cancelled…When I spoke to my oncologist about this, he wasn't too worried: "In the grand scheme of things, Sally, bone cancer isn't going to make a lot of difference." Ha! I kind of love him for that! He's damn right, the lung and brain cancer are slightly more concerning and that's our priority, to get those little buggers and shrink them! If that isn't the outcome of today I will be taken off the current chemo and put on a different drug. I'm rather hoping this one is working, to be honest…despite the side effects, I have energy and feel relatively good and I'd quite like my hair to grow back please…this drug doesn't affect hair—thank goodness!

The brain cancer thing is a battle I seem to face daily at the moment. This morning, there were four posts on Facebook about a girl who ended her life because of brain cancer. I stupidly read the article…don't! I really didn't need to read that and must have more discipline when considering opening links. I've always been bloody nosey though and have severe FOMO (fear of missing out). I know one other person like this, a friend's husband. It's a nightmare—in my head, I'm shouting, "Don't look, don't look," but I just can't help myself!

I have spent this morning cleaning, trying desperately to get the flat shipshape, just the small matter of getting the outside wall fixed and the inside painted again. That and the small matter of NI contributions to sort, Teachers' Pension to sort, Will to sort—feeling a little overwhelmed with it all at the moment. My poor palliative care nurse keeps calling and I'm avoiding the lovely man like the plague. Must call him when I finish this as he is an amazing nurse and I am damn lucky to have the team at the hospice that I have—that place is amazing. I also have a counsellor now, who I adore. I've been told that I hold a lot of upset in my stomach, which could well relate to the loss of appetite…not very good at letting that out sometimes!

Right…time to phone Manolo…dum, dum dum…Much love everyone and enjoy your day!

10 November 2014

A small update but a huge vent! So, St Peter's Hospital has come back to say they are not interested in our TV campaign. They make too much money from the pay TVs. My dad's time in there was just horrendous. At what point should the patients come first…he was in a room with no stimulation and felt awful about himself! I can't believe the hospital does not want to change this, by putting free TVs in their side rooms. I need some thinking time before I write a letter. So saddened by them. Right, chin up, wig on, I'm off to be cheered up by some friends and a sausage! That's not a euphemism by the way and on a plus…I am eating little but more than I was.

13 November 2014

2 a.m. and just back from A&E! A muscle spasm in my back! Can you Adam and Eve it! What a day! Neil Broughton has been looking after me and making me giggle—not helpful when you have a spasm it would seem, but at least I'm smiling. Diazepam and Codine. Looks like I'll be knocked out in a mo! Sleep tight. Sorry, Vickie Bedford and Justin Joseph, for being such a pain in the arse and causing you more work will call you both tomorrow xxx

16 November 2014 The pros of a bucket list!

Spending a wonderful weekend with some of your 'besties' and being able to laugh, cry, drink, snore, moan because your heels are too high and generally have the best weekend! The Sanderson is a remarkable hotel and I would thoroughly recommend it, fabulous service and a complimentary bottle of champagne thanks to my friends' husbands sorting it out. Shopping, champagne, fabulous food at Iberica and a big tick off that bucket list today on the rib boat! I love London, and to go up through the Thames Barrier and speed back with James Bond playing loudly was just brilliant! Followed by a trip to the Tower to see the poppies in daylight. The Sanderson was another tick, somewhere I've always wanted to stay and it didn't disappoint. The best part of the weekend, just spending time with people I love!

So...does the bucket list have pros? Yes! I think we should all have one. Why oh why does it take a terminal ticket to make you realise that every moment is precious and all those things you've thought about doing 'one day', you finally force yourself to do! Another reason, I suppose, to be grateful. If things had plodded along as they were before the summer, I'd have said, "It's too expensive, we'll do it another time." We managed to catch the unveiling of the Liberty window display today and saw the most amazing Gospel Choir, brought a tear to my eye and can't wait to take my godson into town in a few weeks.

The other change this weekend was the wig...I have put the dark wig to the side and gone blonde—I really do miss being blonde. It took a bit of getting used to but it feels more like me. The wig is also real hair, which makes it a lot lighter to wear on my head. Not quite sure how the kids are going to react tomorrow, or even if I'll be brave enough to go for it. I also donned my Chloe heels (thank you Dubai) although those heels were not made for walking around Soho that's for sure! They looked bloody gorgeous though, even if I do say so myself. After two days off work last week, due to a bad tooth and a spasm in my back, I'm feeling better and looking forward to getting back to it tomorrow. I'm also still thinking about how I am going to persuade a hospital that free TVs is the way forward! We will get there eventually and after Christmas, I will have more time on my hands to pursue this properly.

Thank you, Mel, Julie and Liz for a wonderful, wonderful weekend of friendship! We were asked on more than one occasion what we were celebrating and 'friendship' seemed the most apt response, although the dark side of me of course would have liked to say something a little more tongue-in-cheek.

Enjoy your Sunday evening folks, do something you've been putting off and keep smiling.

17 November 2014

How does one give bad news? By telling you that I have a bloody toothache and that is bothering me more than the cancer right this minute! By also telling you that the tumours on the brain seem to be under control and lastly, despite the not-so-good news, I am upbeat, positive and still looking 'on the bright side of life'.

So, the scan results were back and after a call from the oncologist at 7.30 a.m., I hot-footed down to Woking and then Mum and I went to the hospital for our 9.30 sharp (oncologist instructions) appointment. He got right to the point and told me the brain seemed under control, the little critters hadn't grown, and the bigger ones had more calcium deposits which apparently is a good thing! The other critters unfortunately have been working their little magic on me, a couple more on my lungs and a little bit of growth, some new ones on the liver, a few in the lymph nodes (this was evident if they were swimming around—they need some kind of avenue to get to the next place) and lastly a new little one on my spine. This is not so awful because it's small and according to the oncologist is a natural place for breast cancer to spread to. So, the long and short of it, the chemo hasn't been working.

What next? Back at the hospital next Tuesday to have another magic button fitted (portocath—which will make it easier for the new chemo which is intravenous), and then back in on Wednesday for chemo one! The new chemo is not so harsh on the side effects but I will need to look after myself and stay away from illness…not so easy on the morning tube journey when you're being sneezed on; perhaps I need one of those masks.

So, onwards and upwards for the Hitch! Let's see if this new chemo works. It will thin my hair, but hopefully, it will grow back; I'm a little over being a baldie, even though I love my fellow baldie buddies! I was most worried about being put back on FEC-T[13] chemo and losing my eyelashes again. I love my eyelashes…Thank goodness this shouldn't happen—hoorah!

Time for the dentist! Enjoy your day, folks!

19 November 2014

Chemo and the Hair

New chemo one done! Three days of steroids (yukky, yuk, yuk, but will boost my body) and anti-sickness, which I promise you, I will take for the next couple of days. The nurses think I may not need them, but I will have a go without

---

[13] FEC-T is a combination of four chemotherapy drugs used to treat breast cancer. For more information, please consult breastcancernow.org or similar.

when I am a little less busy. Don't really want to puke on students and colleagues; probably not an ideal way to end my teaching career at a school I love working at!

The dark wig has been put back on the block for a while and this weekend I braved the blonde! The school was an interesting experiment. As with the girls on Saturday, I think my colleagues were a little shocked at first…it is a big change, although I have to say, the blonde feels like me and I don't rush to take it off when I walk in the door. The Year 7s were brilliant. They are a lovely bunch of kids and with all my classes I have been upfront about the wig and have kept no secrets…Not because I want to make a big deal but rather to stop the myth that the C word is a no, no. What I have learnt is that people avoid using the W word too, (no, not wanker, Wig…sorry, Mum!). With the kids, it's different. Their reaction was priceless, "Love the new wig, Miss; it makes you look so much more attractive!"

Ha! The year 9s said nothing, in fact, at the end of the lesson I asked them if they noticed the new wig—bless them, "We love it, Miss, but we didn't want to say anything as we thought it would be rude if we drew attention to the wig as it looks so real." The year 11s, "Like your hair, Miss, better blonde!" So, there you have it…a sample of reactions to your teacher wearing a wig, which brings me to my next point.

Is your hair really that important? My hair has never been great, but it's probably been one of my biggest expenditures with designer shampoos and regular colours…In fact, I love my hairdresser who is just amazing. I can remember chewing the fat with a friend and convincing ourselves that we should spend lots of money on our hair…do you remember this Cate

Edwards? It was after a shocker of a bill at Toni and Guys in Richmond!

The first thing that came out of my mouth when I was first diagnosed with breast cancer in 2011 was, 'Will I lose my hair?' Not 'Will I survive?' 'Will I be in pain?' etc…what the hell…my hair! How vain? The day I lost my hair, I cried like a baby and Wendy came and rescued me with my poor dad feeling slightly awkward with two crying girls he's known since they were babies! When it was finally shaved off by Wendy's husband in a barbers full of men (I kid you not), I felt relief…the dreaded was done and it wasn't quite as bad as I thought it might be. Getting it back was amazing and I posted a pic a year ago, pretty much to the day, I was pleased as punch it was back to how it was.

I never worried about my hair in quite the same way after losing it, if it was cut a little short, so be it. If it was frizzy, I pinned it…it wasn't the be all and end all and I wasn't obsessed with it anymore. Don't get me wrong, once those straighteners worked their magic I felt a million dollars, but I didn't need that every day!

This time I embraced the fact I was going to lose my hair and went to the hairdressers had a pixie crop and dyed it bright blonde! And when it fell out, yes I moaned, but I didn't cry, I coped!

So…how important is hair to you? A gorgeous friend with the longest, most beautiful hair surprised me this week by saying she was thinking of chopping it off and donating it to a children's cancer charity, to make a wig. I'm not encouraging anyone to do that, it's your choice, but it grows back folks…it really does!

OK, a small secret…Mine seems to be having a little bit of a problem at the mo…the sides and back seem quite happy to grow back, but the top? I'm looking a little like Alf Garnett…even have the old man freckles! There are prickles though, so keep your fingers crossed. For now, though, it's the blonde! I think they have more fun…

28 November 2014

Well, it would seem I can't sleep before an operation; neither can I sleep after one. It's been a busy old week, GCSE practical examinations at school and rehearsals; a lovely impromptu drink with Stephen, you can't beat a glass of the sparkly stuff in Kettners after a long day; chemo on Wednesday with Neil and then portocath insertion (not a euphemism) yesterday with Mary-Anne. Brought back many memories of Evelyn and a similar incident that happened this time must have something to do with the drugs they use to put you out…(Farting, in case you hadn't guessed!)

It was bizarre marking the GCSE examinations, as these will be the last ones I ever do. Mixed feelings—no more stress but it's sad to think this is the last lot of little people (6ft is not that little I suppose) I will support through a GCSE exam. Brings back wonderful memories of all the kids I've gone through this with…some of who will be reading this now! And also all the great colleagues I've had the privilege to work with over the years. I've been a bloody lucky teacher, have worked with some of the most amazing people and learnt so much from them all.

Chemo on Wednesday with Neil was quite a giggle. The poor nurse who mistook him for my dad four weeks ago and was then utterly mortified because she knew my own dad had passed away and she'd insulted my friend had to face Neil again. The story went around the oncology department and all the nurses were in fits of giggles. Of course, Neil loved the female attention, especially when my Macmillan nurse commented that Neil and I were the same age! Cheek of it! With the highs come the lows though and after a full-on few days, I was a little teary on Wednesday evening…especially when I realised I had a square patch of thick hair on the back of my head! What the hell is that about?

This morning I can see the funny side but Wednesday evening I had a moment…there is no doubt I look like a dick! I also have had a few problems with NI contributions and a threatening letter through the post demanding a huge amount of money was probably 'the straw that broke the camel's back'. Luckily, after weeks of trying, I managed to talk to someone at the tax office yesterday and this little problem was a mistake on their part which has now gone away. God those letters shit you up though, don't they…I half expected the police to come knocking on the door! So, yesterday completed the week with my portocath operation. I can't remember it being as sore when I had it done in Dubai, but I suppose that one came after a wave of operations so I was kind of used to the pain. My 'magic button' was also a tiny little thing you couldn't see…this one looks like someone's planted an onion bulb in my neck…let's hope it's the swelling! The good thing…Dr Dolce is a looker and always makes the whole process much easier, not nearly as personable and caring as JC, but a looker all the same. At least, the poor veins in my left arm will get a well-deserved rest now; my arm and hand are black and blue from needles. Unfortunately, due to the mastectomy in 2011, they can only use one arm now and the veins enjoy hiding from those pesky needles.

Today is a day of rest…can you imagine the anxiousness in my body knowing all the sales are going on? Good job, I'm not driving these days. Although saying that, I did a sneaky bit of parking for Mary-Anne yesterday and I loved being behind the wheel again…naughty girl! I have to be careful though if this onion bulb is to go down and quite frankly, I'm walking around the flat like an old person! Have a fab day and weekend, folks.

5 December 2014

Feeling a little sorry for myself today. After not feeling particularly chipper and picking up some horrible cough/sore throat bug—I blame the tube. I am again off work (you all know how much I hate that) and have had to cancel my bucket list trip with Niamh to Brussels for the Christmas Markets! Absolutely gutted beyond belief. Normally, I would soldier on but the risk of infection and things getting worse are so much greater because of the chemo. I tell you folks…cancer sucks! So, rest for me today and the weekend, hot drinks, crap TV and a promise to look after myself! On a more upbeat and happy note: Well done, Giselle Tomaszewska and Adam Tomaszewski, on your half marathon this morning for cancer research! So proud of you both…I couldn't have done that when I was well!

25 December 2014

Dear all, I just wanted to say Merry Christmas and a great big thank you for all your love and support over these past difficult months. I know both Mum and I couldn't have gotten to today without you all. Now go eat loads and have a fabulous, fabulous Christmas. I absolutely promise to get back to the blog and have my computer packed and ready for the United States bucket adventure!

Big love!

I wouldn't say we're quite ready for the airport! Got to get my wig on!

31 December 2014

Standard evening conversation over here in Washington, DC, a child a few miles away has died of the flu and a woman has gone through Heathrow with Ebola! Ermmmm crapping myself a little one might say! Try not to get paranoid Hitch and don't breathe in public!

6 January 2015

Day 172 since diagnosis and I'm still going strong. What to do when one can't sleep? Make a cuppa and get writing!

It's been a pretty tough month and apologies for not writing more often. When I'm facing things matter-of-factly (not sure that's actually a word), I find it easy to write. When I'm dealing with things on a more emotional level though I tend to be a bit quieter and find it difficult to put pen to paper—or fingers to keyboard as the case may be!

The beginning of December saw me leave my wonderful buddies at Latymer and retire from teaching. While planning all of this I thought I'd be celebrating, instead, I found the whole process quite hard. Giving up work is something I'd never contemplated before; I had just ploughed on through. It worked perfectly at Latymer though as my contract came to an end, so it was the perfect opportunity to finish. My head of department made the loveliest, most generous speech (not sure it was all deserved) but can you save it for the future please Justin…you made me sound great, Do you think you might be able to read at the funeral one day in the future? The pension is welcome now I'm not working but this too took me by surprise. Instead of the celebratory cheer, I found myself in tears…I think it's a reality hit, and the pension is a reminder that I have terminal cancer, something I don't particularly want. I try hard every day not to say, 'It's not fair'. There are thousands of women with this God-awful disease and I'm in no position to moan. The pension is a little like death money though—that sounds dreadfully morbid, apologies; it's a reminder though that I'm sick and quite frankly I prefer to think of myself as fit and healthy…kind of.

Christmas was hard but made all the better for going away. There are days I miss my dear old dad terribly and I wish I could just call him, hear his voice and mull over some of these things that are going through my head. He was good at that was dad, he didn't offer many opinions but would listen and sometimes laugh at me being pathetic—obviously calling me 'mate'…Dad was good at putting things into perspective! Flying on Christmas Day out to the USA was probably one of the better decisions Mum and I made. The distraction of duty-free, the club lounge (oh yes!) and being on an A380 in the Upper Deck in Business Class meant we didn't spend Christmas moping around. Yes, we missed Dad, but we managed to have a giggle and get on with the day. America was fab! Time with Emma and Sarah was precious and new memories formed…

We are so lucky to have this friendship and little changes between us. We still giggle over the same things and I will be forever grateful that 26 years ago we met while watching the boys play football outside Queensmere House! Mum and Emma's mum Jean formed a firm friendship, which was lovely. Both have lost their husbands to cancer and it was great to see them talk so openly about what they miss etc. It was also great for Mum to see how active Jean is and I think it's planted a few seeds in her head of things she might like to do over the coming years.

The worst thing about having a lovely time is the goodbyes…that niggling doubt that you might not see those people again, although the way I feel at the moment, that's unlikely. What is for sure though, is I won't be going back to the States. £3000 it cost me to insure myself…for a week people! There was only one insurance company who would do it and before you ask, I phoned every recommended Macmillan insurance company on their website, all supposedly cancer-friendly! In the words of my very wise, eight-year-old godson, "People with cancer shouldn't have to pay for insurance, Aunty Sally, they have enough problems already!" He'll go far, that boy, mark my words!

So, it's my first week of not working and so far so good! I had a good eight and a half hours sleep yesterday which is probably why I'm wide awake at the crack of dawn today (actually it's not even light outside). I'm not looking forward to today though; we are scattering Dad's ashes. I thought I was emotionally mature up until this summer, I've realised that's not the case and I actually find stuff like this quite hard to deal with. It's not something I ever thought I'd be doing…not yet anyhow. I just thought my parents would always be around. It really goes to show how precious each day is. We're scattering most of Dad's ashes at the crematorium where my grandfather and Nanny's ashes are. We're saving some though to put in the Acer at home when it's replanted, that way Mum can have a place to reflect and we know Dad would like that. His garden was everything to him and if Mum ever decides to move, she can take the Acer with her. I sometimes wish there was a book for all of this…Do you say anything when you scatter someone's ashes, do you sob, do you giggle…? I'd like a guidebook please: A dummies guide to losing a parent; a dummies guide to facing terminal cancer? They're missing a trick, I tell you! Well, one thing's for sure…you'll be hearing a lot more from me now I'm not working!

I couldn't let you go without a quick toilet update: London Underground—I beg you to install toilets at all your stations. On a recent surprise breakfast visit to see the lovely Jo G, Danny and Kerry in Shoreditch I felt a 'Bridesmaids' moment on the tube…you know that sweaty uncomfortable feeling that there might be some action down there and it might come quite soon? Well, I decided to get off the tube (sensible you might think) at Bank station. I tell you, people, do not get off at the Bank if you need the toilet. Sweating and running in an extraordinary position I eventually found a sign for the exit and after wiggling on the escalator found a TFL man, "Is there a toilet nearby please?" I was actually crying at this point!

"No, love, the nearest one is exit 8, there's a Mcdonalds on Cannon Street." Just to make this clear, it had probably been the best part of ten minutes since exiting the tube at this point, I now had to find bloody exit 8, both my shoelaces were undone and obviously bending down to do them could have caused the inevitable to happen. I have never in my life wanted to pull my knickers down and squat in the street like I did right then. A failed attempt at asking a security guard if I could borrow a loo in a nearby office block and asking the local road workers if they had a portable loo meant I could hardly walk down Cannon Street when I eventually found it! I did get to McDonald's, how, without having an accident in my pants is beyond me! Needless to say, I arrived in Shoreditch in a taxi, a sweaty pale mess! My advice to you would be: If you think you might need a number two, do not get on the tube and if you have to exit the tube for said toilet activity, avoid Bank station like the plague!

Have a wonderful day folks!

8 January 2015

Don't judge me as I had this done during my first bout of cancer, but I'm desperate for a good cosmetic eyebrow tattooist. Can anyone recommend one? Bloody radiotherapy combined with the chemo has meant there is hardly anything left and as good as I am at drawing them in, I'd like to be able to have them done soon before I lose any independence. Any advice would be most welcome folks! My lovely cosmetic tattooist who did my nipple too (bet that made the boys snigger) is travelling the world lucky thing! Thanks, peeps!

12 January 2015

The scattering of Dad's ashes was not nearly as awful as I thought it would be. The men at the crem did a lovely little service, although they nearly gave me the giggles with their stereotypical funeral voices and posture, coupled with the long black coats. The other thing that totally surprised me was the amount of ash! I don't mean to offend or be morbid, but the urn was like a watering can and when the man at the crem twisted the top, the ash came out like watering a garden! Dad would have been very impressed! But it went on and on and on…I said to Mum, "There's quite a lot of ash mum."

"He was a big man," she replied. Again, I got a bit giggly, you may think this inappropriate, but I know Dad would be giggling with us. His ashes were scattered with his parents in the South Keep of the crem by a tree with a bird box, amongst the daffodils and crocuses…He'll be happy about that. And mum has kept some for the re-potting of the Acer, one of their favourite plants in the garden.

Chemo came and went. I have a weak ring finger at the moment and my left leg is a little funny which worries me. I told the nurses and will tell the doctor this week. I'm either paranoid or know my body well. I am being careful though and like an old lady, holding the handrails and just minding myself a little. It's a weakness and I think probably now I'm not working I'm losing my exercise (can solve that) and perhaps a little confidence! Who knows! I also lost a toenail…vomit inducing I know! I think this is probably a side effect of the chemo. Don't worry though folks, I'm still smiling and determined to keep fighting these little critters who think they know me so well!

Tonight was fabulous. I have just been to see DV8's 'John' at The National. Those of you who know me from old will know I have followed this company since they started and I could have sobbed at the end for having the privilege of seeing them perhaps for the last time. I don't think it's their best piece ever (who am I to have an opinion) but it moved me like every DV8 piece I have ever seen and been influenced by. This company have probably influenced most of my teaching and myself as a theatre practitioner and for that, I am eternally grateful! Thank you, my darling Latymer, peeps for taking me with you tonight.

Writing this on the phone is a nightmare and so I must finish. The man behind me on the train is eating marmite twiglets so loudly I may shout in a minute and the predictive text is doing my head in! I blame the brain tumours.

Good night, folks and keep smiling!

14 January 2015

Damn 24 hrs. in A&E! It doesn't matter if it's the TV, a magazine—it seems everyone's cancer has spread to the brain! Having not had the 'bestest' of days I should probably be turning this right off! It's like a car crash though…you can't turn the damn thing off! What a sad story! Bloody brain mets!

I spoke in length today to the doctor about the weak finger and numb leg. It seems I was right to worry and by 4.30 p.m., Mum and I were in St Peter's waiting for a full body scan. I suppose the upshot of this is…whatever the outcome. And as Dr Ralph said, the earlier we see what's wrong, the more options we have! Some of the most dreaded words were used today, 'you must rest', 'you must take it easy', 'we need to get you back on steroids' and finally 'have you thought about a walking stick?' I shouldn't complain there are people far worse off than me, but a walking stick and loss of independence scare the shit out of me!

The upshot of the day is that I have my shiny new phone…and it works! Hoorah! And the transvestite who did my scanning today (I kid you not), gave me some wig advice on my way out! Mainly…'your blonde wig is a bit shit, love; get a dark real hair one which will suit you better!' Hahahaha!

Loved him! I tell you what though…she was the demon needlewoman/man (I'm confused) though and did the business in ship shape time with no pain! I'd go to her again in a shot! Sadly, they can't use the dye in my port so it's the old-fashioned arm job!

Thank you to everyone for all the lovely calls and texts today. I was a bit overwhelmed with everything in all honesty and turned the phone off for most of the day. Please don't be offended, it's not that I'm not pleased to hear from you…I just sometimes need a little time to get things sorted in my head.

My lovely mum bought me an extra Christmas present today…a new Hoover! I am so excited about using that tomorrow. We had a little giggle as we chose the beautiful Dyson and I said to Mum, "I've just realised…you're as excited as me about this Dyson as you know it'll be yours at some point." Actually, love that fact! This makes me realise I now need to dedicate some serious time to getting all my affairs in order and a big fingers crossed I'll be well enough to go to Istanbul on the 7 February! It's gonna be fab Neil Broughton!

The man on 24hrs on A&E sadly died! I'm not giving up on this fight though…and if I have to have a walking stick, it's gonna be bloody lovely! Stephen Johnson, get designing!

Live your life, smile and enjoy today you lovely, lovely people xx

21 January 2015

Well, I'd like to be telling you all lots of good news this evening, but as suspected the little critters seem to want to play around in my body causing all sorts of mischief! I've never been one to do things simply; maybe this is another example of that.

So, the long and short of it is as follows—excuse the bluntness, but it keeps you all up to date:

- Brain Mets, slightly more swollen on the right side, hence the problems on the left side of the body. There are, however, a few more little critters that have decided to join them…as if 13 little tumours doing their business in there weren't enough!
- Lung mets, well these are good news and seem to have stopped growing, this makes sense.
- As my chest has felt much better—ooh eer, Mrs!
- Liver mets, yep, growing and being added too, the critters obviously like my liver, reckon,
- It's the champagne!
- Bone mets, yep these are growing and a few more springing up too! Little sods!

There you have it folks…the simple version (the best in my opinion) of what's happening in the Hitch body! As the oncologist said though, there are more options and no one's giving up at the moment. In all honesty, when they tell you that you have 13 tumours in your brain, you kind of know that five to ten years is out of the question. The main thing now is to keep my confidence up, not always easy when you're off balance a bit…which brings me to my next piece of news.

Old lady Hitchcock is now the proud owner of a walking stick. A black one with pink flowers on it, that folds into my handbag…Who'd of thought I could rock the walking stick? It is there just in case, so the likelihood of you seeing me using it is slim unless you're trying to nick my seat on the tube or you annoy me and I feel the need to hit you with it—it's like a kung foo stick.

I explained to the doctor today that I was being very good and only going up the ladder when someone was in the house with me. I thought he was going to choke…turns out I shouldn't be going up any ladders! Oh, peeps if you visit, you have chores to do I'm telling you!

On the whole, the week has been good though and very therapeutic. I have thrown out university notes, lesson plans, you name it and feel a massive sense of lightness, and it's so good to get rid of all the crap. In fact, tonight I am sorting two bags for two little girls with hair grips and make-up etc. I think Lana and Bella are going to be smiling when they get these two little packages! I've also had the loveliest phone message from my godson just telling me he loves me…yes, I wept!

My counsellor gave me the most amazing book to read this week…all about dying. It's something that has kept me awake of late. As I've said before, there are no books and no one to tell you what happens. This book is fab though, it talks about burials, the Egyptians, and you name it! I know it seems a bit odd, but I'm mildly fascinated by the whole thing and am interested. I mean, you don't get married without having some thoughts in your head; you don't have a party without organising it…Why should you die without a little bit of planning and understanding? I sound wrong in the head, don't I? Sorry if I offend…I suppose you could say…it's like a little project and as Mum so rightly put it…there is an end.

Know that I am upbeat, happy and bizarrely as it sounds feel pretty good! What that's about is beyond me; cancer has got to be the weirdest, most annoying thing in the world. I'm bloody thankful for how I feel mind and seem to be getting on ok with the chemo. A new chemo will start next Wednesday.

A little ditty to make you smile…I like to look at chemo a bit like Slimming World! I get weighed every time I go and have a little cheer when the weight comes off! Wrong, but totally the right attitude in my mind.

Big hugs everyone, keep smiling and in the words of one of my ex-pupils who lost her battle against cancer when she was only just 16, 'Every Moment Matters' xx

23 January 2015

Day 195…nearly at the 200…pretty good going I reckon!

So, it seems sleep has eluded me for now. There is obviously a lot going on in that little brain with its ever-increasing critters and that and the mating season for foxes in the park opposite have woken me. It's not all bad, I have been dreaming heavily over the past few nights and I'm not sure quite what this says about me, apart from the inevitable: I'm slightly mad, but I have woken up two mornings in a row giggling to myself! Nutter! The night before last I had eaten a lot of vegetables during the day (good for the relief of chemo constipation…too much info?) and I woke myself up with the loudest most impressive trumps! Now I know this is not to everyone's taste, but those of you who know me well will know how much I was giggling to myself. Anna Bishop, Sarah Hamm, Michael Cooper…I know you are laughing!! Last night I dreamt I was a primary school teacher…Ermmm, what that's about is beyond me. But at 5 a.m., I awoke giggling again as the class had got all their jumpers muddled up and were all saying the funniest things! Any dream readers out there? All I can say is waking up with a smile is not such a bad thing…It does put you in a good mood and at least as a retired old granny I can have an afternoon nap should I need it.

It's mornings like this that I am so thankful for my friends far away out there, as I know that some are up and about their business. How blessed am I to know, if I needed to, I could WhatsApp and have a little chat. I have Izzie, family and friends over in Australia and New Zealand who are awake when I should be sleeping and my girls in the States who are around for those late-night moments! Dubai, who are always up and busy when I wake up early. Makes you realise what a rather delicious world we live in and having friends around the globe, although we miss them dreadfully, is a positive in life! Especially when you're not sleeping!

Last night, Wendy and I celebrated our 45th birthday at the local Italian. 45 years we've known each other and still giggle as we did in primary school. Five years ago we were celebrating in Dubai dancing to cheesy 80s tunes…this year we were drinking prosecco and singing Happy Birthday, not only to each other but to the other people in the restaurant with birthdays! Positano's in Surbiton is such a fab place and if you're ever in the area pop in, you won't be disappointed. It was a good night and as always, despite everything going on in my body, I still feel like me…with a wig!

I also had a lovely catch-up on Skype with The Bish yesterday…I miss our cups of tea and general insaneness and ability to laugh at all the wrong things! It would seem that lovely little Aya and I need a hair swap! She has a lovely curly section right down the centre of her head, while Aunty Sally has a lovely curly section all around the side and is still bald on top! I am desperate for more hair growth on the top…this downy bald look is not good! So not good...as a result, yesterday was pretty much spent wig-washing and clothes-washing! Freaked myself out when I went to the bathroom and saw a head in the bath! Forgot all about it till I heard Wendy scream as she encountered the same in the evening! Ha!

Bucket list Brussels this weekend, rescheduled from December when we had to cancel due to that awful coughing virus I picked up. My first time on the Eurostar and a lovely weekend with Niamh...very excited! Neil and I have also booked Istanbul for a long weekend at the beginning of Feb. It would seem long weekends are to be the way forward for the moment, due to the treatment cycle. There are longer trips I'd like to do, but we shall see. I will make the most of all the opportunities and for the moment, do those little things closer to home. When faced with your own mortality, it's amazing how the little things can make you so happy. A couple of you have asked to share my blog with people, so I've now made it public which I think means anyone can share it or read it. It is personal and I'm sure not appealing to all, but the option is now there. If it brightens one person's day, makes them laugh or feel better about themselves, then I'm happy.

Well, as I'm awake, I think I might do a little bit of yoga to get me stretched and focused...ready to sort that tax! Have a wonderful day, folks! Xx

27 January 2015

What a day! Some absolute opportunists decided to try and break into Mum's house today. The idiot/s threw a vodka bottle through the kitchen window and then couldn't get in because Mum had locked the window! Go, mum! The evening was spent with the police and the forensics…that was quite exciting, and the policeman was quite easy on the eye too, so not all bad. And the best thing…they've been caught and are currently in custody! Good job! The idiots robbed the Co-op in St John's first thing, and then went on their rampage…losing their nicked vodka bottles on the way it would seem! Can you Adam and Eve it? There are days when you think, 'Really…is this really happening to us?' Thank you to all our neighbours and friends who have helped tonight!

The problem with days like today is that it makes me worry so much for Mum when I've gone. It's the bummer of being an only child I suppose, but I know you will all adopt Mummy Hitch and make sure she's ok and looked after. Mum seems ok though, especially as they didn't get in! It would seem poor Chelsea the cat has come off the worst and is absolutely terrified poor thing, and I'm here tonight with my stick should anyone want to try it on. The people who tried this must be so unhappy—karma will bite their bum I'm sure! Either that or Dad will be haunting them right now.

On a happier note, I had a fabulous weekend in Brussels with Niamh and had the best birthday—thank you, everyone! I was truly overwhelmed with well wishes, cards, presents…I can't thank you enough. It makes me quite teary…in a 'what have I done to deserve such love' kind of way? I'm not fishing for compliments here…I am merely saying I am absolutely bloody blessed and lucky to have you all in my life…seriously lucky!

So, another day of firsts ends for the Hitch family! 43 years my parents have lived here and not once have anything like this happened! Got my stick handy if he wants to come back. Again, makes you realise how precious each day is!

31 January 2015

203 days since diagnosis! We're in the 200s...surely got to be a good sign!

I am now 45! How the hell did that happen? Not moaning...always good to see another birthday.

This week has been filled with bucket list highs and little cancer whip lashes to remind me my body is going through somewhat of a change that it refuses to let me ignore!

I had the most wonderful time in Brussels with Niamh. As only Niamh could, our hotel was amongst some of the best designer shops in Brussels and opposite Louis Vuitton, so our arrival was met with much 'oooohing' and 'aaahing' at shop windows! Actually, we should both be rewarded for not giving in to temptation, something in Dubai I'm sure we would have found a way to rationalise in our heads. If you fancy Brussels for a weekend, the Sofitel was just fabulous and the food and cocktails to match...would thoroughly recommend it. Sunday was filled with sightseeing and lots and lots of chocolate! We did a fair bit of walking and despite being a little slow I did manage it! My balance is slightly out of kilter at the moment and so bannisters and dare I say my stick, have become my friend...well kind of!

In all honesty, I didn't use the stick in Brussels, but I did see a very trendy, good-looking guy at the Eurostar (about my age) with a stick and he was rocking it, which gave me a little boost! The new chemo started on Wednesday and we have all our fingers and toes crossed that my body lets this one work its magic. This will be my fifth type of chemo since 2011 when I was first diagnosed with primary breast cancer and I have to say, from hearing the most horrendous stories about chemo I have been lucky! I'm not sure how, or why, but I'm obviously in some bizarre way ok with it. I have invested in a 'Nutribullet' which has become my new best friend! I love it! At least I know I am pumping my body full of nutrients and that surely can only help things. I had a good look at the Macmillan advice leaflet for this chemo and one of the side effects is numb hands and feet, so I'm kind of hoping that this might be why my balance and feet have been a little more difficult to manoeuvre over the past days, we shall see. It's either that or my body screaming out, "You may feel fine, Hitch, but remember I'm still here!'"

So, here it comes…the bit in today's blog I was trying to decide whether I should keep to myself! I seemed to have developed this bloody awful problem of needing a wee desperately at a moment's notice! So, on Thursday, I went to Waterloo to meet my friend Lisa for a lovely afternoon tea at The Library Lounge in the gorgeous Marriott. As I got off the train I knew I needed a wee, but stupidly decided to top up my Oyster Card first. As I did so I was obviously wiggling away like a child and the man next to me was looking at me as though I was slightly unhinged! That's fine; I can cope with that bit! I then had to get to the toilets. This was no easy feat as by now I knew the wee was well and truly on its way…the only way I could get to the toilet was by stopping at every free seat along the concourse and pretending to look for something in my bag—yes, like a nutter!

When I eventually made it to the toilets (the wee was coming by this point), I then had one of those awkward moments when you can't pass someone and they keep going the same way as you and I full-on pissed myself! Not a little dribble…a full-on wee on the floor in the toilets at Waterloo station! Oh, My God! Mortified, does not even come close! I then had the embarrassment of having to tell Lisa what I'd done, buying new knickers and trousers at Waterloo, cleaning myself up and having afternoon tea with a pair of wet trousers in my bag! By the time I went home, the stick was well and truly out…my body had decided to tell me that planning and preparation was now in order for every trip out of the house. If you are out with me and you need spare knickers or leggings…I'm your go-to girl folks! The afternoon tea was lovely though and thank god I was with a friend who made me see the funny side of what will now be known as 'Waterloo Pissgate'. I have mentioned the constant urge to pee to the doctor, but it doesn't seem to be linked to anything. Maybe the sad case is, I've reached middle age and sadly am going to need wee stops more than normal…if that's possible!

As I mentioned, the stick had its first airing on Wednesday. The legs just weren't doing as they were told and my balance was all over the place. It was probably a little to do with the chemo, a lot to do with the fact I had exhausted myself with the 'pissgate' incident, perhaps a small amount to do with champagne consumption (oops) and the fact that I must remember to rest occasionally too—although from my main Facebook page, you'll know I'm enjoying every minute and don't really want to stop that. Anyhow, I got on a packed commuter train to come home with my stick in tow and am sad to say, stood the whole way. It was fine; I held the rail with one hand and the stick with the other, but seriously, not one person offered their seat. Not that I'd have taken it, but still…

Yesterday I spent the day at Penny Hill Park Spa with two friends whom I've known for over 20 years. It was magical, felt like I'd had a week's holiday and the upshot is I had six hours of unbroken sleep last night which is pretty good going for me. Paula and Jo spoilt me rotten and I never know at the moment how to say thank you to all the people in my life who are getting me through these trials and tribulations. I said last night over a drink...I kind of feel like a fraud. When I'm sitting there with friends, chatting away, I feel normal...It is hard to believe what is actually happening to me and bar the little reminders of cancer playing with my body and my kind of bald head with its landing strip, you'd think and I'd think there was nothing wrong with me. It's a funny old disease.

Why Dad and I got it, is sometimes beyond me. I met an old friend on the train the other day who had no idea about the cancer. It was the first time I had to tell someone for a while. He asked what I was doing and I said, I'd retired due to ill health...of course, the next question was did I mind him asking why? So, I said, "Oh, I have advanced breast cancer and they can't cure it now." I then said, "Please don't feel sorry for me though...I'm happy, I've done more things than I could have wished for, I've fulfilled my lifetime dreams, been an actress and a teacher; I've travelled...Things could be a lot worse—I could have been bloody miserable, not done anything I wanted to do and then had to face this!" I then got off the train and proceeded to piss myself! Ha!

Have a good day, folks!

2 February 2015 Note to self:

1. 3 a.m. is not ok to be awake! I blame the bloody cough!
2. It is absolutely not ok to read scary blogs about brain mets at this time!
3. Brain mets can cause incontinence—terrific!
4. My leg not working properly is not good!

On the positive, I'm rather sprightly and might get some jobs done! Always good to make the most of it! Or maybe I'll try another hour of sleep...

4 February 2015

207 days since diagnosis and welcome to what has probably been my longest session at the hospital so far. Thank goodness I had Wendy with me to make me laugh and giggle!

So, it would seem I have developed a new nickname: Wonky Donkey! This is due to the dodgy walk I have developed! I used to love 'Wonky Donkey' so I can live with this one for a while—thank you, Wendy! I spoke to the breast nurse at length about the past week's excitement i.e. 'Waterloo Pissgate' and the inability to walk properly. Lisa, my breast cancer nurse is a pretty amazing lady, supportive, funny and takes on board your worries. At the suggestion of a wheelchair, you can imagine my face! This has huge implications for me and of course, would mean selling my beautiful flat and of course literally losing my independence! Not great right now...even though these little critters are bugging me I'm not ready to throw the towel in just yet—especially with my new eyebrows!

Anyhow, after Lisa talked to the oncologist, I was asked to go and see him. I thought and I think so did everyone else, that the wonky donkey limp had to do with the brain…it seems this may well not be the case though, rather a problem with the tumours on the spine. This would also explain 'Waterloo Pissgate' as if the tumours are causing problems on the spine, it would also mean I might suffer from incontinence. Not great, but better than problems with the brain—there is also the option of radiotherapy to help with this, something my dearest dad had and as mum reminded me 'you might start shitting yourself as well'…thanks, Mum! Ha! So, what next? I have a big MRI scan tomorrow on the spine and if I can manage to stay in the scanner, the brain too…oh and a nice sedative to stop me having a panic attack in the machine. Apparently, the machine is a big one though and most people are fine with it…fingers crossed!

Mum had her other eye done today to which Aunty Ann and Uncle Tony took her, so she is housebound and can't drive at the moment. There are days when you've just got to keep smiling.

I probably won't know a lot more about this until I get back from Istanbul next week. Off on Saturday for a long weekend and am very excited! It's been on my wish/bucket list for the last few years. I'll be in Neil's safe hands and as he says, "If we need to get you a chair, we will," I'm hoping the stick will do the business, we shall see.

When I finished my meeting with Dr Ralph today and put my bag on my shoulder, he said, "What the hell is that? Sally, your bag is massive." Ha! It has a pocket for my walking stick and I love it. It would seem though, that I'm going to have to go for the old faithful black bag that I can carry across my body for this trip, at least I'll have two hands to hold onto bannisters with! Sunday, I had my eyebrows tattooed and I can't tell you how pleased I am. There is no doubt they're a bit out there still and will fade over the coming week, but my goodness, it is so nice not having to pencil them in every day and the lady who did them was just fab!

Thank you so much, Caroline Hanman, for the recommendation. I met a lovely group of girls at chemo today, bizarrely who live up the road, here in Surbs. We had a good chat about wigs though and I'm going to book an appointment at Shepperton Wig Studios who apparently make some fabulous real hair wigs. I think it's time for a new one to add to the collection and as I said to Mum, "If I'm going down, I'm doing it in style!" I had a catch-up with Manolo at the hospice today as well, (he's helping me apply for a Blue Badge which I can of course use in friends' cars). I told him my plans about the wig and it was lovely to have a discussion about feeling good and how that helps the whole process. What with my new Nutribullet, lots of healthy eating, new eyebrows and the possibility of a new wig...however I feel (which is actually not awful), I will not look like I'm ill— there is no need!

So, folks...wish me luck for tomorrow...perhaps wish Cate a little more luck as she's coming with me and those folks in Dubai know that the MRI was not my friend out there—sorry, Cate...I actually crawled out of one...no lie!

Sleep well, everyone.

6 February 2015

209 days since diagnosis and the decision has been made! I will be taking a wheelchair with me to Istanbul! If you'd told

me a week ago this would have been the case I would have had none of it. The right leg is all over the place though and falling in a heap on the floor every now and again is just not helpful, I would be mortified if this happened at the airport tomorrow!

Nothing is ever easy and now I have to send all the dimensions of the wheelchair, etc. through. The scan went ok, well, I stayed in it for over an hour…slept the whole time except when they kept telling me off for moving! Oh dear! The sedatives I had were mad…I was totally out of it!

Well, wish me luck folks…Istanbul, wheelchair, stick, camera…here I come. Poor Neil Broughton…what a hero you are!

9 February 2015

Oh! I so wanted to be giving good news! Sadly Neil and I are coming home…It's ok; we haven't had a horrendous falling out! I got the news yesterday that despite hoping that the naughty leg and ridiculous need to pee all the time were related to the spine tumours rather than the brain, this wasn't the case. The bloody critters on my brain are yet again out in force, so it's back to whole-brain radiotherapy for me! Oh, and a text to boot…double the steroids! Hello, fat face! Not the best news and after much discussion and a few tears…the decision to get back to Blighty to be on the safe side was made. The good people at BA have changed our flight for us so we've only lost out on the hotel. Istanbul is beautiful and the sights are amazing…There is no denying that, but wheelchair friendly in the pissing rain this city isn't, and as the rain looks set to continue for another 24 hours we probably would have struggled anyhow. Oh, how I wish these legs were working…thank god they behaved in DC, NYC and Brussels!

We had a little incident to make you laugh today. Neil fought the cobbles and we did manage the Big Bus Tour! Two hours without the loo saw us race down the cobbled hill…Neil in pain because he needed the inevitable number *two* and me holding myself in desperation for a wee. The pair of us was not a pretty sight! It's like we've become old people overnight! It's a bloody good job we have no airs and graces and can laugh at each other I tell you!

On top of that, I read a fabulous article in *Elle* about a cool, trendy superfood restaurant over here and booked us in! That too went tits up as you couldn't reach it from the roadside so therefore it was impossible for me to get to it with the stick, chair and general weather! So back we came to the old town with possibly the loveliest cabbie in the world. Thought the poor man was going to cry at our misfortune. We did find a lovely rooftop restaurant though and were able to chew the fat over a rather lovely bottle of Shiraz. The main man hates any kind of selfie (hence lack of pics) sentiment or slushiness but Neil Broughton, you are my hero! Thank you!

So, back to the hospital on Wednesday and let's see what the plan is for the radiotherapy! I'm thinking that this is going to put a dampener on some lovely catch-ups I have planned; I'm sorry if that does spoil things. It might well be I have to go on Sally watch again for a couple of weeks! Damn, these brain mets…little critters ruining my bucket list activities. Fingers crossed for the radiotherapy though and bollocks to moonfaced! (Sorry, Mumm but you know that moonfaced is not my friend). See you all back in Blighty and have no doubt

I will be devouring plane food like it's going out of fashion. Make the most of the working limbs folks!

9 February 2015

I have an idea for my bucket list! All I need you to do is familiarise yourselves with this…rest of the instructions to follow. It's going to be exciting and I hope to create a lovely and funny memory for us all…Enjoy, it's one of my all-time faves! Am obviously computer illiterate and can't copy the link! Stay with me on this…its Heaven 17's Temptation!

So, we're going to make a video! And it's going to be full of happy things. You can do whatever you want to Heaven 17's Temptation. Use the original version—it's on the MOS 80s Mix Album.

Here's a little advice:

1. Record the whole song…lip sync, so no need to record yourselves!
2. Get together with others to make it easy i.e. the Dubai guys, the Chi guys, the Latymer peeps; you know what I'm saying.
3. Get the kids involved…that includes you Lois, Mel, Max, George, Ben, Bella, Lana, Isaac, Jonah…the list is endless but I'd like as many of you involved as you can manage.
4. Film yourself the landscape…Think pop video, try and have the phone/camera steady…perhaps on a tripod if you can.
5. Move the camera in and out.
6. Send us your stuff and we (that'll be Jonathan Blake helping me) will edit it all together.

7. I know it's a big ask but you will really be making a special memory…I'm going to get the oncology team at the hospital on board and hopefully some of the wonderful women I meet there on a regular basis…too many inspiring people to mention!

Thank you, everyone…these critters are getting me on a daily basis so no time to waste. It is you guys that get me up and make me brave each day—don't forget that!

14 February 2015

Had a lovely lunch in Kingston yesterday with the girls and was looked after by Mel last night! Thank goodness! The legs really are playing games and sad to say I think I probably would have been scared stiff on my own. Also, just lovely to chill with one of my besties, eat lovely antipasti and watch DVDs…perfect!

Got my radar key yesterday too! For those who have no idea what this is, it's the disabled toilet key and what a find. When you're mobility-bound and need room for sticks and a wheelchair in the bog, this is a godsend! Got chatting to a woman outside the disabled toilet in Bentalls (as you do) who pointed me in the right direction and I was able to purchase one from the management suite at Bentalls rather than ordering online. Instant access for £3 and I can use all the disabled toilets now in the country including the one at Waterloo…goodbye Waterloo Pissgate! Thanks, Jo Barnett for suggesting this! The key is a mahoosive mind…ha! Still getting used to the wheelchair and the stares…and people cutting me up! Thank you to all of you who are basically caring for me at the mo, taking me out and helping me to feel as normal as possible at a bloody time like this…I think I'm still quite reasonable company…just best to lay off the food a little to make the pushing easier! I blame those bloody steroids, but as the oncologist says, if they work—fab. So, despite my moaning, I am trying to embrace my even bigger and better moon face and not make a fuss! The purchase of a new beautiful wig from Shepperton Wig Studios has helped this and I promise to selfie it at some point! It is the best wig I have owned and feels like my hair!

So, a week's whole-brain radiotherapy starts Monday alongside the chemo. I've been warned it's going to be a difficult week and I have to rest so I'll be with Mum for most of it…sleeping and trying my hardest not to feel sorry for myself and grumpy! I will also be doing my exercises and bringing back my 'Kill Bill' attitude to do all I can to get some mobility back in this leg of mine. Being able to walk again would be just brilliant and give me some independence back!

Am hoping the Blue Badge will come through this week too which will make parking easier for those poor people who are ferrying me around right now!

Spending Valentine's with Vickie Bedford (Vickster) today and tomorrow, watching The Bridge Series 2! Can't wait—we so know how to rock 'n' roll and then an evening with my very own hero tomorrow who has promised me if the 27 stairs are too much, he'll carry me! Yeah right, Neil Broughton! Slowly and steadily I will conquer them, just might need a push-up and a pull-up occasionally and perhaps I could go down on a tray. Happy Valentine's, lovely people! And big heartfelt thanks to all you wonderful people who have looked after me this week! That includes you, Mummy Hitch!

Especially when you've caught me lying on my back like an upside-down turtle!

15 February 2015

First video in! Katie Rowley Jones, you!

Thinking end of February for cut-off date, although I know the Chi team are on the 1 March! Chloe McAdam and Lisa Marcantonio I absolutely love you! You made me cry when I opened this…oh my goodness, you are both so kind and thoughtful and I love every single one of these. The Wicked song makes me cry every time…and totally is my mantra…I am so lucky to have been changed by all of you for the better! Sending you much love from Blighty! Love ya lots and thank you from the bottom of my heart!

16 February 2015

Three videos complete and the most amazing surprise from Sharon Dean! Martyn Ware from Heaven 17 has done a video too…I kid you not! I am in absolute awe and what a lovely, lovely man! Yay! Get videoing guys! There's some great wigs and dancing going on! I love it!

22 February 2015

224 days since diagnosis.

Dear all, sincere apologies for the quiet time, but this week has been a little more difficult than I thought. [14]Besides the radiotherapy and the chemo, which has made me tired but not 'ill ill', I have had to face up to the complete loss of

---

[14] Obviously Sally didn't think she had three legs but this has been kept in as a genuine 'Sally slip up'.

movement in one leg and a bit of a loss in the other two. I am without doubt a 'wonky donkey'—wheelchair-bound for the moment and can sadly do little without people around me. In turn, I feel like I've lost some of my dignity and of course my independence. Those who know me well know how frustrating this can be. I am normally a fidget—up/down/up/down, doing things while watching TV etc. To ask to be taken to the bathroom…well, you can probably imagine!

Don't get me wrong…I've had some good days. A fabulous evening with Jo, Mark, Josh and Uncle Geoff on Tuesday; a trip to Caluccio's with Charley and Mum; a lovely day on Friday with Mel, Cate and all the kids…even though the service in Café Rouge was shocking beyond belief! Had a trip to see '50 Shades of Grey' with an introduction to sweet and salty popcorn courtesy of Wendy—so in the grand scheme of things it's not all doom and gloom…more adjustment and hoping the radiotherapy helps the leg! They've told me it will get worse before it gets better so I have to trust them…and in the meantime, the face continues to grow! Ha! If the bloody steroids work, well then, I can cope with my moonfaced!

The hospice has been amazing! I do not know what I would do without their support and help, providing me with everything I need at this difficult time. Three wheelchairs, a zimmer frame, crutches (these are pretty redundant now), and a commode (I kid you not…welcome to my glamorous, glamorous life), a frame on the toilet, grab rails in the bathroom…The list is endless and lots of advice and support which is just what I need. I don't mind telling you, this week, at times, has been petrifying. I've had a couple of falls and not being able to get up is frightening. Needless to say, the pressure and burden on Mum has been a lot. I should be looking after her, not this way around—it's all a bit wrong right now.

Another good thing to be positive about is that Mum has finally succumbed and bought herself a new car. A lovely Nissan Juke, ex-demo. She got a great deal; it has everything on it and I know she'll be safe. This has been as important to me as I want her to be off visiting friends, going to all the garden shows and living her life and this will enable her to do this. Another tick off the list so to speak. There are plenty more ticks I want to make though, so please, please, please, positive vibes for the leg, so I can accomplish some more of my bucket list...

This afternoon I'm off to Stephen and Paul's for some 'Cards Against Humanity'...just what I need and definitely a game to stop you thinking about yourself.

Enjoy the rest of your weekend folks, unless you're in Dubai, then happy first day back...Thursday will be here before you know it!

Loads of love.

22 February 2015

Today has been so lovely! My gorgeous boys, whom I was supposed to be entertaining in my flat this evening, wouldn't let me cancel because of the critters so recreated the evening at their house near Mum. The boys helped me go to the loo, lifted the wheelchair...you name it! How I deserve friends like this is beyond me and despite everything, I feel like the luckiest girl in the world some days! Stephen Gittins, Paul Jones, Ian Reeves and Tony Read thank you from the bottom of my heart for the most fabulous day, fabulous friendship and your love and care! I love you boys so much!

24 February 2015

Don't forget your videos folks…tick tock. If you haven't already done them, the last minute of the song is good…as is all your dancing! Hoping to edit end of next week and v. v. excited. Sorry for the lack of blog, but needless to say I have experienced things this week that would make your hair curl! It's going to take a while for me to formulate into words. I had no idea such medical problems existed! Joanne Marie Taylor, you would not be impressed!

Keep smiling, folks and keep your wonderful videos coming…they are making me chuckle away.

25 February 2015

Another interesting day. Just when I think I'm in for an easy one! Ha! The legs are being very naughty and refusing to do anything I want them to. Frustrating, slightly annoying but lucky enough to have some great friends who are willing to pull up my pants…I kid you not! And these are not nice pants folks—I seem to have lost every bit of dignity I ever had! Well, I could cry—I have cried, but I've decided to laugh in the face of it from now on! I am shying away from posting a pic though. After a long talk with my amazing Macmillan nurse Lisa, we spoke to my oncologist and after chemo, I was whipped down to the MRI scanner for another emergency scan. This really wa a scan with a difference though. The whole point of it is to double-check the spine again. All the problems I'm having seem to be linked to this area and the oncologist is determined to make sure nothing has been missed—hence I was in the machine for an hour! The Dubai guys will understand the problems with this (I crawled out of one when first diagnosed and had my only ever panic attack).

The last one was bearable as they gave me a sedative, but due to the rush of this, it was sink or swim—or not as the case was to be. They prepped Wendy Di Felice who was with me today and allowed her to come into the room with me. So, while I was in the scanner, Wendy gave me a head massage and a leg massage! All the bits sticking out. It was the most relaxing experience! I swear this is the way forward! How bloody lucky am I to have a friend do that for me? So now we wait…if they do find something, they can treat the spine and in turn, I might see some improvements to this pesky leg—yay! If they don't…well then, I have to accept it, hope the brain mets settle a little and hope and pray for a little miracle. I've never sugar-coated what is happening to me, I knew the minute the brain was involved things could become difficult, I did however, possibly naively, think I had time on my side…let's hope that is the case!

I'm also looking at some possible rest time at the hospice. Maybe in their day centre, meeting other people going through the same thing and giving Mum a well-deserved break! I can also have some complimentary therapies, I will find out more when I speak to Manolo on Friday. Maybe I could be the entertainment! I'm sure I'll make a few people giggle! So, there you have it…no stone unturned! We are where we are and I'm determined to ride this shitty week through with a full face of make-up and my lovely wig! I still refuse to look ill…I don't feel in any pain and I certainly don't want Joe Bloggs feeling sorry for me (not actually sure who he is but you get my drift).

Sleep tight all…it's been a long day!

27 February 2015

Thank goodness for Dr Ralph and his insistence to have that emergency MRI! The scans came back and his initial thoughts were correct. One of my pesky brain critters has taken a nosedive into my spine and is pressing down on my spinal cord, hence the mess I'm in from the waist down! I'm no doctor as you know but it's something like this. Although not good in the grand scheme of things as it means another little spread, there is some hope. And the man with the clout who I am so grateful is my oncologist, got me scanned and prepped yesterday ready to start emergency radiotherapy today! All in the hope of saving my legs! So yet again…yesterday was mainly spent at the hospital. My poor body has probably taken a little more than it can handle these past weeks. My core strength has diminished, the legs can do nothing and as a result, I am reliant not only on my poor mum, who is quite frankly knackered, but neighbours and friends too. Transferring from a wheelchair to the car was pretty good until yesterday—now even that small manoeuvre is difficult—thank god for the Petrie family! And a visit from the lovely Melvyn at the hospice—bet he didn't bargain on seeing my sexy pants when he popped round to see Mum yesterday. I've lost every bit of dignity I ever had. I know…I didn't start high on the scale!

The other life change yesterday was that I now can't get up from the sofa so have had to sit on the 'chair of doom!' (Said with a Newcastle accent). I shouldn't really call it that, but as Dad got frailer, he had the same problem so we bought him this chair. I so hated seeing him in it as it's the kind of thing you find in an old people's home…so we nicknamed it 'The Chair of Doom'. Talk about karma…now I'm sitting on the bloody thing and know my dad is having a right giggle up there! What with that, the commode and the incontinence pads—don't any of you moan to me about not having a boyfriend right now ok! So, an appointment with Manolo this morning, followed by radiotherapy this afternoon. It's all go in the Hitch house again! It's never bloody ending, but if it saves my legs—then it's worth every inch of effort I can muster.

Big apologies to people; I've had to cancel plans with these coming weeks. My head is desperate to be the social butterfly, but my body is fighting me every minute on this one for now. As a very good friend pointed out yesterday…it's time I let my body have a fighting chance at this and lack of sleep and doing too much won't help! In the words of Arnie…I'll be back! (Not quite sure where that came from).

1 March 2015

So, another little surprise day yesterday! As I've told you all, things have been deteriorating and on top of this poor Mummy Hitch has developed a virus, which in turn has knocked her for six. In an ordinary world, I could have looked after Mum, made her food and helped her out. Sadly, it seems Mum and I don't live in that ordinary world right now and hasten to add, without the full-time care, Mum was giving me, we got ourselves into a bit of a pickle. Jo Barnett was marvellous as you can imagine—I know you all talk so highly of her and she dropped everything to come and sort me out Friday evening and Saturday morning! I think Saturday morning frightened me beyond belief…It's the first time I have not been able to get my positive thoughts in order and I could do nothing but feel really bloody sorry for myself. I am literally reliant on full-time care, something I have never had to experience. And on top of that, it shouldn't be my 71-year-old mum looking after me…it should be me looking after her!

The outcome—I was admitted to the hospital and am being very well looked after by my wonderful oncologist who came in on his day off and the bloody marvellous nurses at Mt Alvernia who are helping me beyond belief! I have a physio coming in and boy is exercising my upper body to keep my strength going (this has just been an added bonus as Tracy at the hospice has already been working her magic on me too, so with a two-prong attack things can only progress right?) I think my poor body; with a week full of brain radiotherapy, chemo and now a week of spine radiotherapy, is feeling a little weary, so this time in the hospital will be good. It will give me the rest I need…three wheelchair changes to get to the car has become pretty impossible and I am knackered before I've even started the day. The time here will also give Mum the rest that she so desperately needs right now.

So, the plan: Stay in hospital till Wednesday while they complete my radiotherapy to the spine and try and save those pesky legs of mine! Then on Wednesday a possible transfer to the hospice for further respite. Oh, it's all go! Although I want to tell you there was nothing funny about yesterday and I shed more than a few tears—there was!

1. "Sally, are you pregnant?"
"No."
"Shall we do a test?"…erm have you looked at me…do you think anybody has been near these incontinence

pants—oh dear god, if I was pregnant, there would be some miracles going on round here, I tell you! Ha! I blame the steroid tummy.

2. Have you ever peed in a bedpan? No, me neither! There is an art to this and I'm going to pre-warn you all should you ever have this heinous experience. Go slow…take your time and don't push a fast one out. There I was in the middle of my bed creating the 'pissing boy from Brussels'. Oh, the shame and the poor, poor nurses who had to sort the atrocious mess out. I told you, I've lost every ounce of dignity I ever owned!

3. I have possibly the best view of Guildford you could ask for from my bed. It's beautiful and I can see for miles across the Surrey hills.

4. The Banana Board! Look it up. I hope and pray none of you have to experience what I'm going through but if you do…this is just the best invention ever!

5. The food is good.

Good luck to all of you involved in the Surrey Marathon today—Liz Maye's sponsorship coming your way! For me—a bucket list weekend that had to be cancelled. Little Venice in the rain might have been a bit pants anyhow Tania Newton…let's wait for legs and sunshine, plus a visit and cuddle from Devon is in store for me today! I can't wait!

Get better soon, Mummy Valerie Hitchcock, there's no one moving everything on my side table and you know how Dad and I loved that. Have a good day folks and appreciate every step you take today!

1 March 2015

My Godson's hope for the future chart! Yep...I'm in pieces.

2 March 2015

Thought I was having a good day! Uh oh...must have fallen asleep—woke up peeing the bed! FFS...what next? The poor nurses here! I am an absolute mess. Have a feeling the catheter might be closer than I think. Note to self Sally...do not congratulate yourself until the day is over! Been moving one leg, doing my physio, strengthening my core—you name it! Pissing the bed was not on the plan!

On the upside, I have downloaded the London Grammar album—beautiful! Sleep tight folks—sharing is caring and all that.

3 March 2015

The catheter is my friend! Getting plenty of fluids inside me and not having to call the nurses all the time.

I thought I'd get loads more sleep and woke up feeling all refreshed to look at my clock to see I'd had 2 and a half hours! Oh dear! I did manage another hour with the soothing tones of London Grammar but have now succumbed to the iPlayer...poor Rose on Mr Selfridge. I think, *Today, I will be doing a lot of dozing!* When I'm not practising the banana slide, doing my physio exercises (which I'm kind of enjoying) and having my radiotherapy. All good and all to help me get strong again—I'm not going to argue! I definitely feel a lot more positive than I did yesterday and a visit from my lovely Macmillan nurse Louis was the icing on the cake. Laura and

Manolo are working hard to make sure things are in place and I'm bloody lucky to have them in my life.

I'm so grateful we raised all that money in Dubai with the Macmillan cake sale and the hospice is SO grateful to you Adele Minter-Bradley for your recent efforts. I think I need to get my ideas hat on for an annual fundraiser but I'm thinking more Dubai styli…They certainly know how to do it and it could also be a time once in the year when all of you can get together. One of the most wonderful things about this blog is you guys coming together…don't think I don't know you're not all chatting to each other on the phone! It makes me dead happy—excuse the pun! Have a think peeps!

On another note, the videos are just brilliant beyond belief. I have been laughing, crying…you name it. Keep them coming for the next couple of days Jonathan Blake is in NYC but I'm hoping Paul Jones and I can start collating everything, it'll certainly take my mind off the critters for a while.

As mum posted…I'm one of the lucky ones to have support from friends all over the world. And I'm feeling those positive vibes big time right now!

Hope you're all sleeping soundly.

4 March 2015

I'm now settled at Woking Hospice and it's looking like I'll be here for at least the next week, possibly more. There is a lot of improvement to be made before I can go home and at the moment, I need the care. Anyhow, you are welcome to visit but there are a few rules…

1. Every day I have physio and OT, which is very important to my recovery…so if the girls turn up, you

will have to busy yourself, nip into Woking, go make yourself a coffee in the day room etc...It's lovely here and everybody is welcoming.

2. I also see the doctor every day and they will be with me for about half an hour so the same as above applies.

3. The people here are all volunteers and they make cakes for all the visitors, so I thought it would be nice if you all could help out a bit. Think of it as The Great British Bake Off. If you come and visit bring some cake with you and drop it into housekeeping...you will make a massive difference.

4. There's a fridge so if you want to bring some lunch with you etc. please do...there is already a bottle of Prosecco in there...a glass won't hurt!

5. The hospice folk are keen for me to have visitors and keep my life as normal and upbeat as possible.

6. Friday morning I have a very important meeting so that's out, I'm afraid.

Right...with that strict teacher chat, I've probably blown any visitors big time and will be spending my time watching the TV! It's prob best to let me know if you are coming, just in case there's someone else here then.

A couple of little things for you to think about: How do you poo lying down? How do you poo without having a wee? Can you see I'm having a little trouble with my poo? Yep, dignity is gone completely today. Again! The suppository is on its way as we speak!

Go, poo people! And enjoy that feeling!

5 March 2015

So, it's in the darkest of hours you have to face your demons…I'm in the hospice and of course, apart from the very awful experience of losing my dad, I have not come close to death for a while. It was inevitable that I was going to have to face up to this and tonight I have had to. To listen to a family grieve is just awful and how the nurses here do what they do is beyond my admiration. But it has brought things into perspective for me. We are sure of two things in life…being born and dying—what comes in between is up to us. Some people are taken too quickly and there is no time to say goodbye, others have chances to do things, put things in place etc. It's a funny old thing in this life.

Tonight has made me realise I have a lot of fight in me yet…and despite getting my affairs in order there's a fair more bucket activities I want to do.

I am still convinced that the media are missing out on this. 24 hours in the hospice would make great viewing…not in a sadistic way but rather the obscurity of smiles, laughter, tears, and families…there is so much that happens in this small building!

I'm on a listing mission:

1. I don't want any of you worrying about me here. I had to face these demons at some point and tonight I have so thanks for letting me share.
2. Don't forget your cake.
3. I'm still having a bit of trouble with *you know what* which isn't helping me sleep tonight.
4. If you visit tomorrow and I fall asleep on you, you probably bore me.

5. Can't wait to start working on this video tomorrow.

I'd say goodnight, but fear sleep might be out of the question for a little while.

Thank you for letting me write and share these things with you…it helps me more than you know…

6 March 2015

Sharon Dean and Lynn Hilton, you legends! Thank you girls! Love this! How lovely of him to take the time and thank you for sorting this…how do you know him?

Evelyne Matafonov you have just made a whole host of people smile, especially me! Thank you from us all at the hospice!

9 March 2015

Valerie Hitchcock

Hi, all you wonderful friends,

I have to tell you our darling daughter is really not well at present. Those critters have taken hold good and proper. She is in the hospice and being well cared for in this wonderful haven. At present, no visitors but all your prayers and good vibes, please. I will keep you all updated, my love and thanks to you all.

9 March 2015
Sally

Hey, gorgeous people. I've seen the start of the video and it looks amazing! Now we have clips everywhere and with the week of complications I've been having, I am finding it hard to stay on top of it all. Could you merely comment below with your name and I will hunt them out or I'll ask you to email them. Please don't email till I ask though otherwise, I'll be overloaded.

This is so exciting! Xxx

10 March 2015

Valerie Hitchcock

My dear gorgeous friends,

This is the hardest post I have or will ever have to do. My darling daughter lost her brave fight today at 10.30 this morning. She died peacefully without distress and fear, she is now at peace. I shall be calling on you all to help me carry on the work she started. For today, we are grieving but will be in touch in due course. I love you all and thank you for being such a support to us. This did not happen without a laugh, will tell later.

Epilogue—Valerie Hitchcock

When she was younger, I put Sally on a stool at the end of the stage. She asked why she couldn't go on like everyone else. And I said, "Because you haven't learnt enough about stagecraft to go on stage…you need to learn. You can be a runner. You have to learn what it's about before you go on stage."

She auditioned for Annie when she was young. I agreed that she could but warned her not to come out crying if she didn't get it. She had to believe that if she went in there and didn't get it, it didn't matter. So, she went in and auditioned. There were mothers putting their kids in ballet shoes and fussing a load of nonsense. I just said, "Right. In you go." And she did. They measured her first. Well, she was going to be too tall. I knew that right from the beginning. She went on stage and she sang, did the audition. Then they said, "You can go and find your mother now."

So, she said, "Well, before I go, can I have a look backstage?"

That typical cheek was fun. They took her backstage. She got what she wanted! She came out and said, "Can we go to MacDonalds, Mum?"

I said, "Yes. Yes, you can. Come on." She must have been about nine. Yep, about nine.

I think her directness is why she got on so well with kids. You weren't going to get much past her. Fiercely affectionate, but not one to get one over on her.

I know one kid said to me once, "Is Miss Hitchcock your daughter?"

I said, "Yes."

And she said, "She ain't half strict. But she's fair. We do like her."

Sally kept kicking me. "Don't you say anything, Mum. Don't you say anything." Typical.

She'll never go away because of the legacy she left behind, because of situations and lessons and memories. Everything I do and everything I say, still now, I can hear her.

I miss her. It's silly things like missing being able to just phone her up and say, "I went to the theatre last night—you would have loved it, why don't we go and see it?" Like when David and I went to 42nd Street. And listening to *Gypsy*—people use songs from *Gypsy* all the time. Or if I hear *Beauty and the Beast*. Every time I hear that being played, well. They've bought out a recording of *Beauty and the Beast* with *big* singers. So, it's out there, it's popular and it triggers the memory every time.

Humour and how John and Sally used it is also special. No doubt about it. Because when things were black—there was always a funny side to it. My dad, Sally's granddad, was very much a glass-half-full person. Everything could be overcome no matter how bad it was. There was always a lighter side. That's something that I was brought up with and that paid off with Sally.

When she rang us to tell us that she had been diagnosed with cancer, my first reaction to her was well never mind love, maybe it's not as bad as you think. And then, every time, when she was diagnosed terminal—even her oncologist would say to her well never mind, if this doesn't work, I've got something else up my sleeve. He was the most professional old-school pinstripe suit, tie, serious-faced man that I've ever met. You know old-school consultants. Sally goes in there and she makes light of everything and he said to her one day, "What is that around your neck?" and she said, "It's my handbag of course!"

"That's not a handbag, that's a suitcase."

She said to him, "If you had to carry around so many books about your illness as I'd do, you'd have a bloody suitcase around your neck." And he just laughed because she's come right back at him. And then he said he was going to put her back on steroids.

"Noooooooo!" she said, "I don't want a moon face. Don't keep giving me a moon face!" He laughed at that.

Later he said to her, "Do you think it's about time you had a wheelchair?"

"Don't be silly!" she said. "I'm not going to have a wheelchair!"

She had a stick though. She had to have a stick. She needed it to stop herself from falling over; it was a balancing thing. I mean she said of her left leg, "I put it in the bath water and I can't feel if it's hot or cold. I put the other leg in and it's too hot."

She's telling the one nurse this story and I said, "Well that's a bit silly. Why don't you put the other leg in first?" He laughed! The nurse laughed and Sally said, "Oh I never thought of that!"

But that was the sort of silly things that were coming out as she progressed through. She helped people too. A lady came into the clinic—it was her first chemo session and she was terrified. You could see she was terrified. And Karen (who died a year after Sally) said to her: "What's the matter? What cancer have you got?"

"I've got breast cancer I have to have a mastectomy."

"Oh! Sal's had a mastectomy! Piece of cake—she'll tell you about it." So, Sally reassured her.

One of the last things she said before she was very ill was, "Mum, I don't regret anything. I've had a good life. I've done most of the things I wanted to do. I've got no regrets." At least, there is that.

She sent me a text on the Sunday before she died. "Mum, if you've got time." (Fancy saying that!) "Mum, if you've got time, can you come and give me a cuddle?"

And I went in there and there was a nurse sitting with her and the nurse said, "She's frightened." But she never ever told me that. She hid it well. I did sit with her on that last night and then it came to 5 a.m. If someone is going to die during the night, it's before 5 a.m. So, at 5 a.m., I had been holding her hand. And just before 5, she went to sleep. I watched the clock then at 5 a.m. I thought, "Right, we're going to have another day. I can go to sleep."

I went to sleep, woke up early in the morning and she'd put the telly on. "Ooh, you're awake."

I started singing, "Good morning, good morning."

She said, "Shut up! Don't do that!"

The nurse, Elaine Patey, who nursed John through the night, said her internal organs were packing up. So, I knew then that it was close. Just didn't know when. The next morning the doctor and senior sister came in (singing morning!). She took me aside and said it was close. Neil was there with her and we were holding her hands and talking to her. And I told her I loved her. And Neil said we all love you. And the doctor said to her, "You're breathing."—They gave her oxygen—she'd had a job to eat and drink so we fed her crushed ice.

She said, "Yes please," to more morphine to relax. We kept talking to her.

Then the sister said. "She's gone." Pause. And we stopped.

We went out and they put a nice clean nightie on her. And put her wig on. And put some flowers in her hand. Yeah, and she was very peaceful. So, then when we went to see the funeral directors. Sally had already chosen her coffin because she came with me when we registered John's death. John had already said before he died. "When I go and you go to the funeral director, ask if they do two for the price of one."

Sally said, "Are you going to ask them?"

I said, "I might as well."

So, I asked, "Do you do two for the price of one?"

And she said, "I beg your pardon?"

Sally said. "I've got terminal cancer so I might as well choose my coffin now." So, she chose her coffin then when Neil and I went to the funeral directors, the lady said to me, "I know you, don't I?"

And I said, "Yes, I asked you if you do two for the price of one. Well, I'm here."

"Oh my god!" She said.

I swear I got a discount! I swear it!

And then, um, I said that she wanted her Manolo Blahniks on her feet. And she said, "Well when she comes, we'll wash her hair."

"Well that'll be a waste of time," I said. "She hasn't got any!" We just made sure she had a wig on her head!

I came home and got a nice dress that matched her shoes. The last thing I got was her babpapa. A red thing, sort of velvet. She took it everywhere. It was only small and that was put in with her. I regretted not taking it into the hospice at first, but I found it in her bedroom before I took her clothes and knew that had to be in there.

Sally Is Always in Our Hearts

I have raised a lot of money in your honour Sal, from the Al Warqaa coffee morning to doing the 5k walks. I am sure I have more in me. You were taken way too soon and it makes me so aware of my own mortality and how to live my life! Keep on singing love. You will always be missed. – **Anna**

When I'm having a really rubbish day, I think of Sal and know that even in her darkest days she still managed to laugh.

Even though she's no longer here, she still has the ability to make me smile every time I think of her. They don't make them like Sal anymore. – **Niamh**

I definitely had a carefree attitude to everything, including my health and then there was this one day, which I still talk about and which epitomises Sally for her frankness and her absolute care for others, even when suffering herself. She once said to me, "Give me your hand, you need to feel this lump," she gestured to her chest. I cringed at first. I couldn't imagine why I would want to do that but Sally soon verified that for me.

"You need to know what it feels like, in case you ever have the same thing."

I still have never, ever forgotten what that felt like. I check myself regularly now. Prior to that, I never did. It was a tough lesson to learn but I now fully appreciate the importance of regular checks and vow that in the unfortunate circumstance that I find myself in the same situation, I will do the same; women supporting women. – **Adele**

Good friends are like stars you don't have to see them to know they are there…A plaque from Sally I still have. – **Wendy**

When the song 'Happy' by Pharrell Williams came out, we must have been out partying in Dubai somewhere with Sally as I remember her saying, "I love this song" with a huge smile on her face as she was singing & dancing along. Whenever I hear that song now, particularly the line 'clap along if you feel like a room without a roof', I always picture Sally as it reminds me so much of her—she always seemed to live her life in such a positive way—no limits and always going for it, just like 'a room without a roof…' – **Lisa**

I [then] created positive change. I quit my corporate job; I changed my entire career. I turned my life around. Through your loss I realised to be blessed with a life and not fulfil it to its full potential was a life wasted. You taught me so much when you were here with me, and your words have stayed with me. I wanted to do something with purpose that made a difference for the greater good, and this was all influenced by you. I love you; I think of you,

I miss you so very much, I am grateful for all that you gave me. – **Izzie**

236

Sally played a part at our Civil Partnership on the 6th October 2007. It was a massive surprise to her friends, all a big secret, and she played Mazeppa the stripper with the trumpet in Gypsy! It was brilliant!

In January 2013, Sally was teaching in Dubai... Tony and I smuggled her into our hotel room to get changed before we went out on a boat to a fancy restaurant for supper. Whilst we were all getting ready, we spoke about her book, she told us she wanted to make a book, a legacy, and we threw around some titles....she had a pet name for her cancer, it was something she laughed about, lived with, and something she really didn't want, but was stuck with. Like having someone turn up at your party who you really didn't want to have there – The Uninvited Guest – BOOM, that had to be the title of her Book...

Sally was a force! – **Ian**[15]

[15] Heartfelt thanks to Ian for collating and printing Sally's blogs initially and for creating the memory page *sallyhitchcock.muchloved.com*